UTI THE SAMURAI SWORD

C.M. GRAHAM

Clarence Graham's spellbinding story of heroism, capture, survival for three years in Japanese slave labor camps and witnessing the atomic bomb on Nagasaki is another "unbroken" - how the will to live was a force far greater than all the atrocities he suffered. Read it and be inspired. Read it and be proud to have him as a fellow citizen.

Tom Brokaw

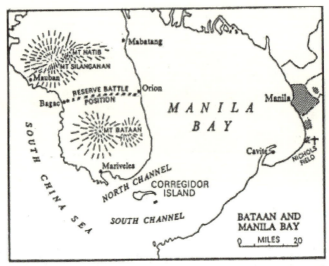

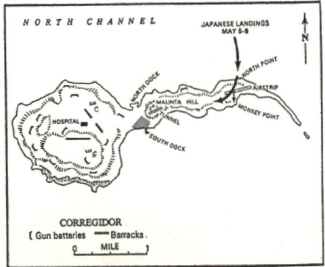

The Silent Drums

I fell on my straw mat, tired and sore,
A helpless and sick prisoner of war.

As I closed my eyes, I could see
A group of dead soldiers, in front of me.

They marched to the beat of a silent drum.
The flag they carried was tattered some.

My heart beat a rhythm to their unheard band,
"I salute you boys", and I raised my hand.

With ghostly faces and eyes straight ahead,
They were only a part of the millions dead.

A vacant space was in their ranks.
One motioned me in, but I said, "No thanks,
I haven't received the call".

C.M. Graham

Acknowledgement

It was with encouragement and push from my family and friends that finally caused me to write this book. I am indebted to them for their confidence and help. I give special thanks to Doris, my good and cheerful wife of fifty-plus years, and to my four children and their families, all of whom I am very proud. To all, thank you.

The author would also like to express his thanks to Jay Hodges, whose outstanding editing contributions were greatly appreciated.

The Author

Author's Note

This is a true story of the experiences of just one military man in his life and death struggle while in the Pacific Theater during World War II, the war that has been recorded as being the greatest and perhaps one of the most tragic wars in the history of the United States. It is the war in which some 55 million died and some 3 million more are unaccounted for. It is also the war in which the United States suffered its greatest and most humiliating defeat - that of the loss of the entire Philippines.

It is not the author's intent to cover the whole of the atrocities suffered by the millions of individuals during this period, but only to relate one person's day-by-day existence during that time.

The story opens with the peaceful and relaxing island life, then carries the reader through the days of intense combat, the facing of the enemy as ammunition and supplies expire, the horrible experience of being captured, the brutal days of torture and slave labor as a prisoner of war and then on to the wonderful return to freedom back in the arms of the United States.

In so doing it gives the reader an insight into that period not covered in most U.S. history. It points out the confusion that led to the "writing off" of the entire Allied forces in that far-away theater. It is this part of history that some of our great leaders would like to forget.

Those who erred are not to be blamed, for we all do make mistakes. It is however, only by revealing them that we can avoid such in the future and hope that it will be knowledge helpful to generations to come.

The Author

Table of Contents

Tom Brokaw

Maps

The Silent Drums

Acknowledgment

Author's Note

Contents

Chapter I: Bataan: A Paradise

Chapter II: Bombers In The Air

Chapter III: Jungle Fighting

Chapter IV: The Death of Corregidor

Chapter V: The Victory March

Chapter VI: Cabanatuan

Chapter VII: The Farm

Chapter VIII: The Hell Ship

Chapter IX: Fukuoka Camp 17

Chapter X: Winter

Chapter XI: The Atomic Bomb

Chapter XII: The Food Drop

Chapter XIII: Number Two Train

Chapter XIV: Back to the Philippines

Chapter I

Bataan: A Paradise

Bits of bright blue sky flickered through the upper canopy of the dense tropical forest towering more than two hundred feet above me. In spite of the near hundred-degree temperature and high humidity, the soft green moss of my resting place was cool against my perspiring back. Lush undergrowth of vines and flowering plants flourished in the shade of these tall trees that stood like ancient Greek columns.

This open area between the jungle floor and the first limbs served as a flyway for beautifully colored parrots, awkward hornbills, smaller birds, and species I had never seen before. From my green bed, I could watch flying insects, such as gaudy butterflies and eight-inch-long preying mantises, and the noisy monkeys in their daily activities, apparently unaware of my presence.

What seemed like paradise was actually the Bataan Peninsula of Luzon, the largest island in the Philippines. The area had been off-limits to Americans in the past because of the hoards of malaria mosquitoes that were known to be there. Little did I know then what lay ahead for me.

I was a member of a U.S. Army anti-aircraft battery that had been moved from the island fortress of Corregidor to the area so that we would be in a position to intercept any enemy flights should war break out. Corregidor lay a few miles south of us, across the north channel of Manila Bay. Here we set up our four big anti-aircraft guns on the highest point.

A smile crossed my face as I watched a little monkey twisting a banana from a bunch hanging above my head. Things seemed so peaceful. My thoughts drifted back to my early teen years on my parents' farm in eastern Nebraska. Those perfect June mornings when I would till the straight rows of new corn with a horse-drawn cultivator and stop the horses more times than necessary to savor the warmth and promise of spring. Sometimes I would imagine a little halo around my shadow's head and pretend that it was a guardian angel. How strange that I would think of that curious practice years later, while watching a monkey eating a banana.

  I recalled my dear mother telling of how once when she was a teenager a terrible thunder and lightning storm came up in the middle of the night. She was so frightened that she got out of bed and put on her best dress so she would look nice if she were killed. She told me how relieved she was when, as she lay there waiting, a white halo appeared on the ceiling above her and the storm stopped. Perhaps I inherited some of her imagination.

Suddenly I was brought back to reality by the loud banging of the alert bell. I sprang to my feet and rushed up the game trail to our gun position. Our battery commander, Captain Abston, was talking in his soft, quiet Southern accent as I rushed in. I remember his calm voice saying, "The Japs have just bombed Pearl Harbor in Hawaii. They will, no doubt, hit here soon. *Man your stations.*"

We had enough of the three-inch anti-aircraft (AA) shells to last two or three weeks, and more would be coming from storage. Food would be stacked and well camouflaged in hiding locations throughout Bataan Peninsula. Since Japan had made the first attack, our government would feel free to send our military forces to bring the enemy quickly to their knees. After all, didn't we have the most powerful navy afloat? And a well-trained army and air force? Only a year earlier, when I was stationed at Fort Riley, Kansas, our ranks were starting to swell with many signing up to beat the draft.

Being young and eager and wanting action, I had asked for a transfer to the Philippines, and I got it. I remember my then commanding officer saying, "Why the Philippines? That's going to be a real hot spot." That to me was the ultimate challenge and promise of adventure in an exotic arena.

My job was to operate the big director, the mechanical brain for our anti-aircraft battery. It would compute the altitude, range, and speed of incoming enemy planes. Our four big guns were synchronized with it. All that the gun crews would have to do would be to match their pointers and cut the fuse when a flight came in range. After Lieutenant Peterie said that the height finder and all guns were ready, all we had to do was wait.

I leaned back against the sandbags. The early sun was warm and comforting. A cool, moist breeze wafted in from the China Sea to our west. Sounds of the jungle around us seemed to blend into a background symphony.

For some reason I began reminiscing about that old bum I had met on the wharf in San Francisco during my transfer from Fort Riley. I could envision his face. What a strange but friendly character he turned out to be. After hitchhiking from Kansas, I arrived at the dock late at night in San Francisco, too late to catch the last harbor boat to the embargo center on Angel Island. I dropped down on my duffel bag in despair. After traveling eighteen hundred miles, I couldn't make the last mile. So there I sat, penniless and chilled to the bone in a dense San Francisco March fog. I wanted to pray but thought better of it. The Lord didn't get me into this mess, so I had no right to ask him to get me out of it.

I was thinking about the long hours ahead when I noticed a man shuffling toward me through the fog. My first thought was that he might be a mugger or a robber or maybe a murderer. His long, tattered coat dragged the ground. His baggy pants were worn through at the knees. A stocking cap was pulled down low over his ears. As he got closer, I saw that his shaggy beard sparkled with droplets of dew from the heavy fog.

A sudden fear wrenched through my body. I was a soldier without a gun. My breathing seemed almost to cease. I could hear my heart pounding in my temples. He stopped directly in front of me and stood there for what seemed an eternity. Finally, in a pleading, whining voice, he said, "Fellow could you spare a dime for a cup of coffee?" I was shaking so hard I was sure he'd be able to hear it in my voice, but I blurted out, "Fellow, if I had a dime, I would buy myself a cup."

A big, beautiful smile lit up his face, revealing a full set of pearly white teeth. "Well now," he said patting the bulges in his front pockets, "we can take care of that. I know a little coffee shop nearby that stays open all night and has good coffee."

We went in, a soldier in uniform and a bum in rags but with pockets full of change. The man behind the counter was fat and jolly. After the bum explained my plight, the fat man said, "We take care of our servicemen here. There's no charge for the coffee, and you can stay here the rest of the night. I'll call you when your boat arrives in the morning."

I woke at the sound of a bell ringing and was told that my boat had arrived. I fell in line to go aboard and then noticed that all those ahead of me were paying as they got on. I got an empty feeling in the pit of my stomach. I stepped aside to let the others go around me. The skipper looked over and said, "Well, are you coming or not?"

"I don't have any money," I replied.

"Your fare is paid," he said. "Come on."

As I turned to pick up my duffel bag, I noticed the old bum standing nearby. His proud grin showed his sparkling white teeth. "Thanks," I said. "How can I get in touch with you so I can repay you some day?"

"Just do what you have to do," he said. "I'll be with you in spirit."

As we crossed the bay, we passed by Alcatraz Island, which at the time was a federal prison. In the heavy fog, it looked more like the back of a gigantic whale than an island. As we docked at Angel Island, our embarking center, military guides with gas lanterns met us. They told us to grab our gear and to keep a hand on the shoulder of the man ahead of us as they led us to our quarters. Not sure I had grabbed the right bag, I felt around until I found my padlock.

Inside, the lights were bright and the area was spotless. Two long rows of double bunk beds ran the full length of the room. I tossed my bag onto an empty bunk and headed for the latrine. On my way back, an orderly from the kitchen instructed us to line up for breakfast.

They had stretched a rope from our barracks to the mess hall, and we were to hold on to it as we went to keep from getting lost. I'd followed it right up to the mess hall door before I could see the light coming from inside. I was so hungry that everything I ate tasted great.

Orders were posted daily for work details and for those who were shipping out that day. On March 31, 1941, almost a week after I arrived, my name came up: "Clarence M. Graham, 800 hr troop transport Republic." The ship *Republic* was a liner that had been acquired from the Germans after WW I. At last I was really on my way.

I remember so well the thrill of sailing under the Golden Gate Bridge on that early morning. However, it was minor compared to the joy of passing under it coming from the opposite direction four years later, after the end of WW II. After a few hours out, the *Republic* hit groundswells, monstrous, smooth walls of water. There must have been at least fifty or more feet between trough and crown. When the old ship sunk into the low valley, it seemed as though it would keep going down forever. Then in the next minute it would rise high on the top of a roll, from where we could see for miles. Soon we hit the swells on the diagonal. The round-bottom ship would roll almost ninety degrees to one side and then back the same to the other side, all while the nose pitched up and down.

I started feeling feverish and prickly all over, and soon I felt nauseous. It wasn't my heart that was in my mouth. I made a mad dash for the railing, and, holding tight to a rail, I fed the fish with all I had in me. I then developed the dry heaves. An old sailor duckwalked up to me and said, "Mate, you better swallow if you feel a hair in your throat, cause that's your asshole coming up." I wanted to jump up and push him overboard, but I was too weak to move.

We stopped at Pearl Harbor, Hawaii, to repair one of the ship's propellers. We thought we would have a chance to see the island and some of those beautiful Hawaiian girls we'd heard so much about, but we were told there'd be no passes off the boat. However, they did bring a dancing team aboard one evening, which was accompanied by good Hawaiian music and sing-a-longs.

En route to Manila, flying fishes and dolphins played at our bow. By night the Southern Cross oriented our direction, and by day monstrous sailfish leapt high from the smooth waters or tail-walked on the surface only to come down broadside, making a showery mist as they disappeared into the depths. As we crossed the International Date Line, tomorrow became today. I spent my twenty-first birthday on the old ship *Republic*. To celebrate I had a can of sardines, a box of crackers and a coke.

Our ship took a somewhat southwest direction, apparently to pick up favorable ocean currents and avoid a storm. As we crossed over the equator, the ship's crew put on a "King Neptune" program, and we each received a certificate that made us members of Davie Jones's Locker. The captain made an announcement over the loudspeaker when we passed over the deepest part of the ocean, the Mariana Trench. "Kinda scary," I remarked as an old, weathered sailor swaggered by. He answered gruffly: "Makes no difference, Doughboy, once it's over your head."

Twenty-eight days after leaving San Francisco, we sailed up through the San Bernardino Straits and entered Manila Bay. We passed the little island of Corregidor, known as the Rock of Gibraltar of the East, or the Rock. It was my destination. However, we sailed on into Manila's pier seven. To my disappointment, it was nothing like the beautiful harbor at Hawaii. It was hot, and the air reeked of filth and rotten fish. Raw sewage and garbage floated in the water around the ships, providing a banquet for noisy and aggressive seagulls.

Looking down toward the dock, I saw the faces of brown-skinned children with very white teeth. They called to us in a language that I had never heard, their arms stretched up to us. We tossed what coins we had, which caused a mad scramble. I found myself searching for the smiling and bearded face of the friendly old bum, but of course he was not there.

Those of us heading to Corregidor boarded a small, open harbor boat. Most were natives who had jobs there. There were so many aboard that the passengers even crowded onto the flat rails. One of the natives who was sitting on the fantail was very drunk and fell overboard into the propeller. The cry "Man overboard!" went up in two languages. Seeing the blood on the water, the skipper said, "We can't help him now. The sharks have him." It was my first experience in how little value is placed on life in some countries.

We docked at Corregidor on April 22, 1941. A small, rugged island that's shaped like a tadpole, Corregidor is nestled in the entrance to Manila Bay. Just two miles north across the deep North Channel is the southern tip of the Bataan Peninsula. There was, at that time, a small airport on the low narrow east end. It stretched east-west between North Point on the north shore and Monkey Point on the south shore.

Farther up the tail to the west was Malinta Hill, through which General Kilborne had begun excavating the famous Malinta Tunnel in the thirties. It was lengthened to about 750 feet with several laterals. The main part was around 25 feet wide and 15 feet high. (It was enlarged much more later on.) From the ceiling to the top of the hill was about 100 feet of concrete, rock, and earth covered with dense low-growth trees, brush, and vines.

Farther west, before the "tadpole's head," the shape of the island narrowed and dropped to near waterline. Here was Bottomside, a base camp with native concessions stands, the motor pool, 92nd garage, and the south dock. Even farther west was the main part of the island, rising to 550 feet at Topside, its highest point. The officers' golf course was located on the relatively flat Topside as was what was then purportedly the longest concrete barracks in the world. An American flag flew on a hundred-foot pole over the nearby main parade ground.

The entire island was covered with a blanket of beautiful tropical flowers, trees, and vines. Halfway down the northern slope, notched into the hillside, was Middleside. It also had long concrete barracks. Each of these barracks had many tall window openings that reached nearly from the floor to the high ceilings. There were full-length shutters to close over these openings during the tropical storms. These shutters were studded with mother-of-pearl-type shells to let in filtered light.

I was assigned to Battery G, of the 60th Coast Artillery (Anti-Aircraft) at Middleside. Battery G had just been formed from old Battery C on topside, so we were the new kids on the block. We were issued wool shirts, which were surprisingly cool when wet with sweat. Not being accustomed to the prickly tropical heat—our constant companion—we sweated constantly.

During an early morning drill on either our second day, our newly assigned commanding officer, First Lieutenant A. A. Abston, called us to inspection arms. He ordered me front and center. I had no idea what was coming. He had me drill the battery for a short time, and then he told me to report to him in the orderly room. After splashing some water on my face and putting on a dry shirt, I reported to him in a proper military manner. He gave me the "at ease" command and told me he had received my records from the States and noticed that I had been in the Nebraska "U" ROTC and the Nebraska National Guard prior to joining the cavalry at Fort Riley, Kansas. He pointed out that I had completed clerical school and had been a battery clerk and a battalion clerk. I knew then what was coming, and I didn't like it.

As a clerk I had sat at a desk piled with papers and service records for both men and horses. From my window, I watched the men riding in drills and mock battles. When he told me that he was making me the battery clerk, I humbly explained that office work was not to my liking and how I had transferred there to see some action. "Well I'm glad to hear that," he said, "so this is what I'm going to do. You set up this office and file system for me, and I'll give you a man to train as battery clerk, and if you train him satisfactorily, I'll put you in the headquarters section on the director instrument."

"That sounds great to me," I said, and that is the way it was.

Peacetime on the Rock was a breeze. We did calisthenics in early morning, had breakfast, close-order drill, and then artillery practice, all in the forenoon. After our noon meal, we had the whole afternoon to do as we pleased, but we couldn't leave the island. There were the Beer Gardens, day rooms, which had games and pool tables, the Post Exchange (PX), and in the evenings some of the latest movies from the States were screened outdoors.

I wandered down to the South Dock one hot May afternoon and saw an old-timer sitting out on the very end of the dock, staring into space. He reminded me of the ragged old bum in San Francisco, until I talked to him. He was bitter and in a nasty mood. I asked him what his problem was. He told me that he was on his third enlistment on this island, his native wife had just left him, their kids were not his, and he had the clap. He said, "You know, on my first enlistment here, I would sit ~~here~~ in this spot and look out over the sea and think of home. On my second I would just sit here and look. Now I just sit here."

"Well," I said, "what are you going to do, jump in?"

"Hell no," he said. "I can't swim."

One terribly hot Sunday afternoon, I was lying on my bunk, watching some little lizards crawling on the ceiling above me. They were great at catching flies and mosquitoes in their upside down position. All of a sudden, a marine clad only in shoes and shorts jumped into the room through one of the windows. He ran across the squad-room floor, climbed out the window on the other side, and took off down the hill. I hardly had time to clear my head before two more, dressed the same, ran through. When a fourth one came through, I yelled, "What do you guys think you're doing?" As he sailed out the window, he called back, "Four mile run." Another one yelled, "Some damn guy didn't make up his bunk!" Their tough training, however, was nothing compared to the reality they encountered later on.

Chapter II

Bombers in the Air

During the first week of December of 1941 our Battery G (Globe) and a searchlight Battery E moved from Corregidor's Fort Mills to the Bataan Peninsula, just north across the North Channel of Manila Bay. We moved all of our anti-aircraft guns, ammunition, small arms, kitchen, supplies, and personnel. Included was a big brand-new radar. It was enclosed in a box-type trailer that had its own power supply. It was one of only two in the entire Philippines. With it came a tech sergeant, who was a well-trained operator. Near as I can recall, his name was Feavyer. He was a nice guy whom everyone liked.

On December 8, 1941, we learned that Pearl Harbor had been bombed earlier that morning. We worked hard, expecting an enemy attack at any moment. In just a short time, we had our anti-aircraft guns in place and well camouflaged, and we were ready for action. We had just settled down with our noonday chow when the roar of an approaching dive bomber brought us to our feet. The enemy pilot apparently spotted our position, banked in on us, cut loose with his machine guns, dropped his bomb, and was gone. Searing shrapnel cut through the vegetation. No one was hit, but a hot, smoldering fragment landed at the foot of one of our more highly emotional soldiers, and as smoke started rising from a bed of dry leaves our man yelled, "Gas!"

Then came one of the most humorous events I can remember from the war. We all were required to have our gas masks on hand at all times, so we kept them in a canvas bag with a shoulder strap. When the soldier yelled, "Gas!"

all gas masks were hauled out of the bag, and with them came a shower of candy bars, cigarettes, cans of sardines, chewing gum, and who knows what else. To add to the chaos—keep in mind that none of us were combat seasoned at that time—one of the men forgot to remove the cardboard covering the lenses of the mask. Apparently thinking it had turned dark because of the smoke and feeling an immediate need to relieve himself, he pulled it out and let fly on the back of a fellow soldier. Supposedly he thought he was peeing on a tree. I think it was the last time I laughed for the next four years.

Needless to say, a free-for-all started immediately. Captain Abston was furious. Not only had no one fired at the plane but also, as he put it, we were "acting like a bunch of f—ing recruits." It was hard to imagine then that these same men would soon settle down and become one of *the* crack anti-aircraft units, setting a world's record for shooting down the number of planes per number of rounds fired.

Then we heard the drone of heavy bombers in the distance followed by the sound of bombs exploding. They were bombing Clark Field, the landing field just north of Manila. Abston and Colonel Breitung, the battalion commander on Corregidor, had a quick phone conversation. They decided that we were to move to the very top of the mountain we were on and set up just above the abrupt drop-off to the North Channel. We would be in the open but covered by camouflage nets when not firing.

The bombing of Clark Field, and Nichols Field two days later, raised havoc with our air defense. A series of miscalculations and blunders followed. Things happened that were never told to the general public. With the loss of our planes and navy in Hawaii and then our planes in the Philippines, we were sitting ducks. Why our planes were once again caught lined up and on the ground is hard to understand.

General Douglas MacArthur was in charge of all U.S. and Philippine forces. He was brilliant in some ways but very conceited. He had been recalled to active duty along with other reserve officers just three months before. His office and residence at that time were in the Manila Hotel. He had been serving the Philippine government as their military advisor in shoring up Philippine Commonwealth Army. When he was recalled, he was the senior ranking officer, and he was appointed supreme commander of all U.S. Army Forces in the Far East (USAFE).

With the rapid escalation of the war in Europe, President Roosevelt and Prime Minister Churchill of England decided that all war efforts would be concentrated against Hitler. Although war with Japan was imminent, the Japanese, they thought, would not be able to start any major offensive for at least six months. Then, and only then, would the Pacific forces be supplied and strengthened.

MacArthur, while working with the Commonwealth Army, had prepared a plan to defend the Philippine Archipelago. The stockpile of food and ammunition—what there was—was stored in warehouses in Manila. Should this plan fail, we were to enact Plan Orange and move the stockpile to the Bataan Peninsula. The Philippine Army of 100,000 men was poorly trained, poorly equipped, and very poorly paid.

The U.S. Army troops numbered only 31,095, and of these, 12,000 were the well-trained Philippine Scouts. All equipment was very much out of date. The tin helmets, Springfield rifles, and artillery pieces—all of World War I vintage—were a weak force to hold off an entire enemy invasion.

Just before noon on the day Pearl Harbor was bombed (nine hours later by Philippine time), a radar station operator at the little landing field of Iba picked up an approaching formation heading in the direction of Clark Field forty miles to the east. Moments later a Filipino vigil on North Luzon sighted and reported these planes were flying in a V formation at twenty-five thousand feet altitude—direction, Manila. A coastal watch reported that there were nearly two hundred planes in the flight. This information was sent to Clark Field by telephone, radio, and teletype. Most of our fliers were at lunch. An aircraft-warning officer received this information and promised to pass it on immediately, but the planes were there before he got around to it. Soon after the message was sent, the Iba radar station and its sixteen P-40s were annihilated by Mitsubishis and Zeros.

One B-17 bomber from Clark Field was patrolling over the Bataan mountain range when the crew sighted what they assumed to be a thunderstorm moving toward the Manila area. However, they ignored it. Three B-17s were on the runway at Clark Field preparing for an observation flight over Formosa. The other planes were lined up in neat formation. The enemy hit in three waves, ending at 1:30 p.m. Planes and field were demolished. It was reported that MacArthur seemed numb through all of this and did not give an order. Historians to this day differ as to why.

We could see the smoke from where we were on Bataan. Soon the first flight came in range of our position. I can remember that the dull drone of approaching heavy bombers brought the entire battery to full alert. Captain Abston stepped up on his bank of sand bags and raised his binoculars. The sun was high overhead. We cautiously slipped on our very hot tin hats. Although our radar was not as yet operational, the four big anti-aircraft guns were ready, including the height finder and the director instrument, the mechanical brain that I would be operating.

The heavy drone grew louder. The very ground seemed to vibrate. The buzz of the jungle ceased. Everything became strangely quiet except for the increasing throbbing of those heavy engines. I could hear my watch ticking as we waited. Then out from a bank of white puffy clouds they came—shining silver bombers in perfect V formations. They were going to come right over us, like a flock of huge geese.

"Get on them!" yelled Captain Abston. I set my crosshairs on the nose of the leading plane, as did the man on the height finder. Lieutenant Peterie, our range officer, watched the dials. "Track even and steady," he cautioned. The wind velocity and direction had been entered, as well as the air density and humidity. With steady tracking, the altitude, direction, and speed of the flight could be computed. All this information would be electrically transmitted to all guns.

"They are at twelve thousand feet," Lieutenant Peterie whispered. "We can reach them." They looked so close in my scopes, but they were still too far out. The powder fuse of our three-inch shells had a maximum setting of twenty-one seconds. I heard Peterie counting: 26-25-24-23-22. I expected him to give the order to fire on 21, but he continued the countdown. "Damn it!" yelled the captain. "What are you waiting for? All guns fire one round!" The lieutenant repeated the command over the gun phones.

In an instant, shells clanked into the fuse cutters then into the gun breeches. Lanyards were pulled and the trajectories were on their way. We waited—and waited. I could hear Captain Kwiatkowski, who was in charge of the gun crews, counting off the seconds. I was counting too but to myself, as I'm sure was everyone else. As my count hit 20, four black puffs of smoke appeared among the formation. The left wing of the lead plane broke away and fluttered down like a leaf from an autumn tree. The rest of the plane started a slow spiraling descent. Another turned off trailing smoke. The remainder of the flight broke up and circled back, soon disappearing into that same bank of puffy white clouds. "Corregidor can breathe deeper this time, well done!" Abston called out. "But let's do better next time."

In the earlier days of the war, only the leading plane had the bombsight due to a shortage they seemed to have had at that time. Due to our shortage of anti-aircraft shells, we were very limited in the number of rounds we could fire at each flight. This never improved.

MacArthur did not put Plan Orange (withdrawal into Bataan) into effect until late December, thinking that his small force could guard and hold the entire coastline of the big island Luzon. The food and ammunitions stored at the Port Area in Manila did not get moved, nor did rice from the rice-growing area of Cabanatuan. This later proved to be a disastrous mistake. By his refusal to move these supplies, as was the secret plan established by our government years before and still in effect, MacArthur set the stage for a starvation situation for the peninsula of Bataan, our last defense area.

When troops pulled back into Bataan there were, by count of our quartermaster, fewer than twenty days rations of rice, thirty days of flour, and fifty days of canned meat or fish. This would feed the eighty thousand troops and twenty-six thousand civilians who packed into the area for less than one month. Also, medical supplies were not moved. Men were dying in the trenches, not only from enemy fire but also from lack of food. We on Bataan were put on half-rations almost immediately. MacArthur was more concerned about his own image than about the advice being given by those under his command.

To supplement our meager diet we sent hunting parties into the surrounding jungle with the dual purpose of finding and eliminating Jap snipers and to gather anything edible to add to our soup pot. As three of us were sitting under a monstrous tree waiting for some grunting wild pigs to move into view, a sort of a muffled "punk" sound came from somewhere above. Our man sitting in the middle jerked backwards. There was a small caliber hole in the middle of his forehead.

It was some time before we located the culprit. He was tied high in one of the tall trees. When we finally got him, he came tumbling down at our feet. It was then that we gained a new respect for our enemy. He had split-toed canvas shoes, cloth leg-wraps, a small shawl wrapped around his waist to keep his belly warm, a suntan uniform, and a helmet. Each of these was camouflaged with fresh leaves and moss. He had a small bag of some kind of dried fruit and a mesh sack of hardtack tied to his belt. There was a canteen half full of weak sweet tea strapped over his shoulder. He had seven shells for his long-barreled, small-caliber rifle. One of these had been fired.

A bounty was issued of two pesos ($1 U.S.) for each pair of sniper ears brought in. The native mountain Igorot and jungle pygmies were great for collecting these. They used spears, machetes, and arrows instead of guns, and were deadly accurate. They could move through the undergrowth like a shadow. At times they would wait by the roadside for one of our cars that was heading to the front line. They would ride without saying a word, and they would hop out before the vehicle came to a stop. Carved up bodies of snipers were found in areas where they had disappeared. Although the sniper hunters were few in number, the Japs were deathly afraid of them. The bounty for ears had to be stopped because some of our Filipinos showed up earless.

We didn't get any wild pigs that day because of this noisy ordeal with the sniper. We did, however, pick up a big iguana and a wild chicken on the way back to our gun position. We caught the iguana by hand, but we shot the chicken with a .45 caliber pistol, so there wasn't much left of it.

As we worked our way through the tangle of undergrowth toward our gun position, we heard the bang of a .45. We automatically hit the dirt. My face landed in a mass of wet leaves, from which sprang a thirty-inch-long snake. It seemed to be more frightened than I, if that's possible. It slithered up over my shoulder and across my back and was gone. I have no idea what kind it was.

As we came into the clearing of our gun position, our plump little second lieutenant, whom we had nicknamed "Two-Gun Hoot-Mix" after two old-time movie cowboys, was standing with a smoking colt .45 caliber revolver in his left hand and another, unfired, in his right hand. He had a scared and sheepish look on his face.

Captain Abston, red-faced with anger, lectured him. We learned that "Two-Gun" had been practicing his quick draw and the left gun fired by accident, just missing the captain. Two-Gun was immediately transferred to cooking detail and later completely out of the battery.

Dive bombers kept trying to knock us out, especially just before a wave of bombers were to come over. This kept our machine gunners busy. Bataan had been isolated for so many years that some of the jungle creatures had grown to an enormous size. As one bomb hit close and uprooted a large tree, out from its mossy root mass came squirming a monstrous cobra. Somewhat confused, it slowly slithered down between the gun number four pit and our range section pit.

Someone yelled, "Snake!" Our man Don Spaulding grabbed the first thing handy, a fly swatter that First Sergeant Kendall had made for him out of an old boot, and dashed down the path. He saw only the center section of the snake as it was crossing. Thinking that it was a large, nonpoisonous python, he gave it a mighty whack on the back. Immediately, the snake's head rose a good three feet above the ground, and it spread its gigantic hood. Spaulding grabbed a garden rake and pushed its head in the other direction. As it started on down the path, one of our gun sergeants emptied his .45 pistol at it but never hit it. Then one of the gunners, using his .30 caliber Springfield rifle, got it just behind the head with one well-placed shot.

After much thrashing around, the cobra finally stopped moving. It was big and heavy and had a large bulge in its middle. They brought it over to me to be measured since our range section had the survey equipment. I measured it with the Philadelphia rod, which is thirteen feet long when extended and measures in tenths of a foot. The cobra measured twelve and nine tenths feet long. When we cut it open, we found an undigested young wild pig inside. On opening the cobra's mouth we found that each of the two poison sacs at the back of the upper jaw was larger than a man's whole thumb and full of an amber fluid. The mouth was a good four inches wide at the base, and the lower jaw could easily be unhooked from the upper. The two fangs, each over an inch long, folded up against the roof of the upper jaw when the mouth was closed and came down at right angles when the mouth was pulled open.

All but the head and skin was given to the cooks. No one asked questions that night when our meager ration of soup and rice was doled out. I did, however, protest one morning when drawing my ration of soup and a monkey's little hairy hand came up in the ladle. After that I always told the cook, "Don't stir it, just dip mine off of the top."

On December 12, a Japanese fleet with troop transports gathered just north of the northern end of Luzon. Five of our remaining B-17s with two squadrons of obsolete fighters were sent up from the south to hit them. But mistaking our cavalry for the Japanese landing party, our planes bombed and strafed our cavalry, annihilating all that were in sight. About half of the cavalry was hiding in the nearby woods to function as a second cavalry charge unit. Unseen, they survived the raid.

Soon after our planes wiped out half our own cavalry three thousand enemy troops landed at Aparri, at the very north end of Luzon. General Wainwright, who was in charge of the troops in the northern part of the island, correctly guessed that this landing was a decoy strategy and held his main forces at Lingayen Gulf, a third of the way down on the west coast. Three other landings were made down at the south end of the west coast near the town of Mariveles. Men of the navy, marines, 45th Infantry, and my battery repelled these troops. On December 16, two busloads of enemy troops moving south from Aparri were ambushed by a company of Filipino infantrymen and annihilated.

The big invasion came at Vigan, which is just north of Lingayen Gulf. They unloaded eighty-four transports of troops and equipment. Our men, having no air support, being few in number, and weakened by fever and lack of food, pulled back to regroup. Wainwright's men were fighting against overwhelming odds. This was the beginning of the long days and nights of killing and being killed.

On December 21, the enemy landed sixteen more transports of troops that moved down the central plains. On December 23, General MacArthur put Plan Orange into effect.

On December 24, Manila was declared an open city as requested by Philippine President Manuel Quezon even though the U.S. food, ammunition, and supplies were still stored there. He believed that with this action the Japs would not damage the city or the Filipino civilians. However, this was of no help.

Some of the Philippine army were assigned to move the entire stockpile to the Bataan area, but very little ever got there. Much of it appeared on the black market and in the hands of family and friends. There was also some kind of rule in the Philippines that would not allow rice to be moved from one province to another.

MacArthur never overruled this. He seemed to want to please Quezon, who was young MacArthur's godfather.

On January 2, 1942, Japanese General Mashama Homma made his triumphal entry into the city of Manila. Civilians were slaughtered, women raped, property looted, and food and everything of value confiscated. Many were tortured for information.

On one enemy fly-over of heavy bombers headed for Corregidor, our battery put a shell right into the bomb bay of one of the planes just as the bomb doors opened. There was a terrific explosion that disintegrated that plane and took out a plane on each side of it. This word got to the Associated Press news correspondent, Clark Lee. He visited our battery on January 12, 1942, and wrote the news article that later appeared in many newspapers across the United States.

In his report he told of the smooth operation of the Globe Battery, and that they had made a record for number of hits per number of rounds fired. This news report, along with several others, helped inspire the population in the States to cooperate into one big united movement and turn the tides of war in both Europe and the Pacific. On January 15, MacArthur sent out this message: "Help is on the way! Thousand of tanks and hundreds of planes are being dispatched." We wanted to believe this, but we were well aware that all help would go to Europe because the Japanese controlled the Pacific Ocean.

There were relentless air raids and ground attacks by day, and snipers and sneak enemy patrols attempting to slip through our lines by night. All of this is expected in war, but the constant hunger, malaria, dengue fevers, night blindness from lack of vitamin A, and lack of medical aids continued to wear down all of us. The knowledge that we all were doomed added to the strain. By January 20, our front lines were starting to crumble.

Repeated reports from Washington that help was on the way proved to be false in mid-January, when no ships or planes or help had arrived. Washington had decided to abandon the Philippines. General Eisenhower's new war plan left out the Pacific Theater. The commonly held belief was that Washington justified increased military action in the European Front at the expense of the Pacific because "There are times when men just have to die."

General MacArthur was not informed of this decision at the time it was made. Instead they were still sending him word that help was coming. This decision was also withheld from the general public, who were screaming for the government to send help to the men on Bataan and Corregidor for retaliation toward Japan for what they had done to Pearl Harbor and our Pacific Fleet. Failing President Roosevelt and the persuasive Churchill had secretly agreed to this decision. Both President Roosevelt and our Joint Chiefs of Staff lied to General MacArthur. Later, to save their face, they ordered him to Australia.

It was around this time when someone, or several people, composed the following little ditty, which became famous: "We are the Battling Bastards of Bataan, no mama, no papa, no Uncle Sam. No aunts, no uncles, no nephews, no nieces. No rifles, no planes, no artillery pieces, and nobody gives a damn!"

More casualties had begun coming into the field hospitals than the small staff of nurses and doctors could cope with. The Jap dive bombers seemed to be using the big white cross on top of the hospital tent as their bull's eye. They strafed and bombed the tent, knocking patients out of their beds or killing them on the spot. Nurses and doctors, tired and haggard, reeked of sweat and blood. Many of the casualties were suffering from gangrene that had turned tissue to a swollen, greenish-purple, stinking mass. The swelling was so painful and doctors so overloaded with surgery that some of these swollen limbs were just cut open to relieve the pain and pressure. It was a surprise to the medical staff that many of these gangrene patients survived when oxygen and maggots got to the wounds. Improved, the patients would hobble back to their units where they could at least fight back.

Water was hauled to our gun sight in an aging army water tank mounted on an old truck. We filled it from a good well down by the Number One Field Hospital, which was located on the Marvalus–Cabcaban road that crossed north of our mountain. One day I rode shotgun for them to guard off snipers. While waiting for the tank to be filled, I wandered across the road to the emergency tent where doctors were swamped with the wounded.

As I stepped in under the tent flap, my feet sank into the soft, blood-filled earth. Fresh human blood rose up around my combat boots. One of our soldiers was being held down on a table by two big corpsmen, and a surgeon was sawing off his right foot just above the ankle. The leg moved back and forth with each stroke of the saw.

The poor guy was biting down hard on a stick and not saying a word. I knew they had run out of painkillers. The surgeon saw me and said, "Grab that foot and hold it still." As I did, blood oozed up between my fingers, and I could feel the crunching of shattered bones. The foot came loose in my hand. It seemed heavy. I stood staring at it. "Well, drop it in the bucket," the surgeon said. "And thanks! Stick around, we have a lot more to do, and I can use you."

"No," I said. "I got to go." As I headed back to the water tank I wondered which was worse, killing or repairing.

Chapter III

Jungle Fighting

Jungle fighting not only puts the soldier under the usual battle stress but also tortures him with masses of mosquitoes by night and hordes of biting flies by day. In addition there are lice, fleas, leeches, and spiders of all kinds. Hunger and fever are also constant companions. Sleep is not sleep at all but a state of exhaustion. Like a wild animal, the mind and body are attuned to react to any unusual sound or movement. Actual sleep could lead to death. Danger comes not only from the enemy but also from poison snakes, insects, and even some of the spiny and poisonous vines. A combat soldier doesn't have a bed or blanket. He just drops for a moment or more where he is. Drenching rains, chills, and itchy fungus feet are part of the experience.

One miserable night during a torrential downpour I had dropped onto a big log, and in my semiconscious state I was aware of lizards and ants crawling over me. Too exhausted to care, I ignored them until I imagined my log was out at sea and moving on an ocean ground swell like those we encountered as our ship sailed away from the Golden Gate Bridge. I jolted awake when my log, which was sliding down the hillside, hit a tree and dumped me and my lizard and ant companions into a flash flood stream. Groping in the dark, I finally found my rifle under the log, packed with mud. My .45 caliber pistol was still in its holster, so I was still okay. Those old Springfield rifles had a tubular cleaning kit right in the stock, so the next morning I washed out the mud and re-oiled it, and it was as good as ever.

MacArthur made his one trip to Bataan on January 10, 1942. We didn't see him, nor did we want to. We had well-qualified generals with us, and we felt that MacArthur's place was back at his headquarters on the Rock. One of the things that irritated the fighting men most was his boisterous radio broadcasts, called "The Voice of Freedom," about "MacArthur the Magnificent." He had a great talent for making a big success story out of a minor scrimmage or even a traumatic counterattack when, in reality, it was a tragic withdrawal. I guess it was intended to intimidate the enemy, but we were too mad to appreciate it.

He also kept broadcasting that food, reinforcements, and ammunitions were on the way, though by that point he knew darn well that there would not be any. Of course we knew that too. The fantastic rumors that everyone was making up or adding to seemed to help by softening some of the despair.

At dawn one morning when there was nothing for breakfast, three of us slipped down through the dense underbrush to a little banana acreage where Captain Abston, earlier, had bought all of the mature bananas. We were hoping more would be ready. For safety, we avoided the trail, but we kept it in sight at all times. I noticed that the fast-creeping jungle vines, which sometimes grow as much as fourteen inches in a single night, had been recently pushed back.

We approached the little acreage with caution and discovered our Filipino farmer tied to the doorframe of his tiny bamboo shack. Blood from bayonet holes covered the front of his short-sleeve shirt. Big green blowflies had already clustered around his wounds. In front of him lay his wife and their children. They had been bludgeoned to death by bayonets. The muddy trail leaving the murder scene was marked with the familiar split-toe canvas shoe tracks. The family had been completely defenseless.

By this time, the front line was not a front line at all, but an area where our troops and the enemy were intermingled in chaotic hand-to-hand jungle combat. Snipers were everywhere. We had constant guard duty all around our gun position. The Japs were not quiet as jungle fighters, which was a big plus for us. We could usually sense when one was trying to slip up on us.

I relieved the guard one night at the south side of our position. There was a half moon out. Shadows shifted on the undergrowth in the soft wind. There was a steep drop-off down to the main channel below us and an updraft of warm air. The relieved guard headed back to the unit, and I quietly walked over to the abrupt edge, from where I could see the outline of Corregidor two miles away. It was dark except for the flashes of artillery. The waters of North Channel were also black except for a yellow fluorescent trail made by a small boat in its desperate dash for the Rock.

There certainly could be no snipers on that side of me. But as I stood there for a moment I had this strange feeling that someone was slipping up behind me. My bayonet was fixed on my rifle, and my heart was beating so loud I couldn't be sure of what I was hearing. There was a small grassy area behind me, which I sensed something was crossing. I locked my elbow down tight against my rifle butt and spun to the right, bayonet at bay.

There he was, not more than ten feet away, large, and shaped like a fat Buddha, covered with a yellow floral kimono. He sure wasn't one of ours. The shadows from a swaying palm tree gave the appearance that he too was swaying. My first thought was to thrust to his heart, slam the rifle butt into his crotch, then karate chop his neck. But I couldn't tell where his crotch was or if he had a sword or a bayonet. A thin shadow partly darkened the moon.

There was no time to waste. I let out a Yankee yell and made a mad dash with all of my speed and strength. I charged into him, thrusting my bayonet to the hilt in his heart area. Bracing my feet I gave a quick jerk to the left to throw him off balance. But his monstrous weight didn't move. I tried to jerk the bayonet out but it wouldn't come. Pulling back and bracing my feet, I pulled the trigger, discharging my rifle. My bayonet released instantly, tumbling me into a backward somersault. I sprang to my feet again, and there he was, just as before. I blinked my eyes and tried to make out his image.

The thin cloud that had covered the moon moved and my enemy was revealed: a big moss-covered decaying stump. The blooming moss covering it gave off a fluorescent glow, similar to what I had seen on the water as that little boat stirred up the blooming algae of the bay.

"What in hell are you doing, Graham?!" a voice from behind me said, "You scared the shit out of me." The guard I had posted had come to my rescue.

"Oh nothing," I replied casually. "Just a little bayonet practice."

Hunger nagged at everyone constantly. The craving for food made the digestive juices flow, causing painful stomach cramps, irritation, and stomach ulcers. The meager daily ration of a thousand or fewer calories per man (thirty-five hundred to four thousand being normal) was often delayed or didn't arrive. Everyone was constantly searching for both the enemy and anything edible. Food shortage had become another deadly enemy.

I could really relish the dinner now that seemed so repulsive back in peacetime in Manila. Several of us who were new on the Rock got our first pass to Manila. Much of the city was off limits to soldiers at that time, but that didn't bother us. We had heard of a little Chinese restaurant that served a big banquet for just a few pesos. We finally found it in a cellar under an old store in the Chinese district.

The only entrance was through a slanted lift-up cellar door. The old board steps leading down were swept clean, which we took as a good beginning. The dirt floor had also been swept clean. From the six-foot-high ceiling hung a single forty-watt bulb on a drop cord.

The head of the family greeted us graciously with bows and a big smile that exposed large, protruding front teeth. He didn't speak any English, so we made gestures that we wanted lots of food. We smacked our lips and patted our stomachs. He seemed to get the message and motioned us to the table, smiling and bowing. Next he hurried to the little kitchen from which we could hear a tremendous amount of jabbering and excitement. He returned, again with all smiles, wearing a beautifully embroidered, big-sleeved kimono.

Two very young Chinese children hurried out with dishes, little cups without handles, and chopsticks for each of us. Next a young Chinese lady served hot tea. She bowed as she filled each cup.

We had quite a wait, but there was a lot of action back in the kitchen. The teacups were kept filled. Finally, in came the parade of food. One child carried a large bowl of steaming hot rice and the other a big platter of steaming vegetables and little dishes of sauces. Then came the man himself, carrying a large platter with what looked like a little stuffed pig. It had all kinds of sauces and spices on it, and it smelled really good. We dived in, and shortly we were all trying to figure out what animal we were eating. We all agreed that it wasn't pork.

As the old man came by me, pouring more tea, I grabbed him by the coattail and pulled him back. Pointing to the meat I said, "Oink, oink?" He shook his head in disappointment and, patting me on the shoulder, said proudly, "You know, Joe. Meow, meow." As soon as we were outside I lost it all, as did one of the others.

Corregidor was catching heavy bombing and our battery G was scoring some fantastic hits on those flights that were low enough to be reached with our old fuse type, three-inch AA shells. Some of their newer bombers were now flying just above our range.

Early in February one of our submarines made it through the Japanese blockade with a small quantity of modern three-inch ammunition that had high-explosive powder and mechanical fuses. These fuses had a time clock nose on them that could be set in our present fuse cutters. They exploded with a sharp crack and left a white puff of powder instead of the black. They were great and served us well. The only problem was that there were so few of them. After losing a few more planes, the enemy flights started to split and go around us, and then they'd send in their dive bombers and really hit us hard.

On March 11, 1942, General MacArthur left for Australia with a small staff and his family. Other women and children had sailed out in May of 1941, on the ship *The Washington*. By this point the Philippine army had lost nearly all of its officers. Captain Abston called up three of his noncommissioned officers (I was one of them) and asked if we would take a field commission as a second lieutenant and be assigned with the Philippine army. I asked if I had any choice. He told me that I did, so I told him I would stay with our unit. The other two went. The last report we got on their status was one emptied his .45 pistol on a Japanese tank as its machine guns mowed him down. We never heard what happened to our other man.

General Wainwright took command of all forces in the Philippines around March 20, 1942, and moved into MacArthur's headquarters on the Rock. He placed General King in charge of the troops on Bataan. General King had an impossible situation. Food and ammunition were out for many of the sections and the enemy was breaking through the lines in several places. There was much hand-to-hand fighting. And since our men were weak and vastly outnumbered, the enemy infiltrated our front like a cancer.

There was a lull one dark night. No sound of planes, no sound from the leafless jungle, and not even the usual buzz of insects. The quiet was eerie. I realized that we had forgotten how to relax. After removing my sweaty boots and wriggling my steaming feet, I leaned back against the sandbags that surrounded our pit. I thought I would just reminisce a bit. After sitting there for a while, I realized my mind was a blank, that I was sort of in a stupor. Disgusted with myself, I pulled on by boots. As foot number two went in, there was a sharp pain that went through my bare heel like a full charge of electricity. My reflex brought my foot out so fast that my knee hit my chin with a terrific jolt. I pounded my boot against a sandbag and then cautiously reached in. A pair of pinchers grabbed my finger, and I jerked my hand out. A scorpion came out with it and nailed me on the back of the hand. I beat it to death with the heel of my boot.

My leg was paining clear up to my hip. Furious with my carelessness I decided to limp down the trail to where there was some mud in which I could soak my aching foot. The hand didn't hurt nearly as bad. I informed the guard where I was going and why and that I would give a password—"scorpion"—when I came back. When I found a good spot, I pulled off my boot and pushed my swollen foot deep into the warm clay mud.

It was just starting to feel good when I heard a slushing sound from up ahead on the trail. I was hoping it was a caribou, but no. This creature had just two feet, not four. Again my heart started making too much noise. I jammed my foot, mud and all, back into my boot. As I stood up both feet sank deeper into the mud. The sound was quite close now. I snapped my bayonet onto the end of my rifle, and as it seated it made a loud click. The footsteps stopped. I waited. Then a Jap voice said, "*Owhie.*" I answered, "*Owhie.*" There was a moment of silence, and then the voice rattled off a bunch of stuff in Japanese. Since I couldn't understand a word of it, I remained silent. Besides, my feet were stuck in the mud.

    I adjusted my position for the bend in the trail he'd have to negotiate, pointed my bayonet, and braced myself. With a hideous yell, he charged. My bayonet caught him dead center, and his momentum sent me over backwards. He landed on top of me. As he was groping around in pain for something, I was able to pull out my pistol and place a round into his spine. See the enemy first or die.

    I heard other footsteps hurriedly retreating back down the trail. My would-be assassin lay still. After freeing my feet and bayonet, I headed back up the trail. Being too concerned about the bleeding from my left side, I completely forgot about the password. "Halt!" yelled the guard.

In a squeaky voice that surprised even me, I replied, "Just me." Then, bang! A bullet whistled just over my head. "Damn it!" I yelled back, more in my normal tone. "It's me, Graham."

"You stupid shit," he said. "Why give a password if you aren't going to use it?"

"Just wanted to see if you could hit anything," I replied, "and now I know you can't."

Our most dependable warning system was Captain Abston's little dog. He was a little, short-haired, white terrier-type mutt, and he could sense the approach of heavy bombers long before any of our outposts could. He would crawl onto the lap of the closest person, and in his shivering state would invariably urinate. We called him Radar. I can't remember what his real name was. Abston liked him because he was such a friendly little fellow, and being top man is a lonely job.

One morning Radar was missing. Most of the men in the battery searched and called for him but Radar didn't appear. It soon became apparent that the men of one of the sections were unusually unconcerned about him. I don't think that Captain Abston ever found out what happened to Little Radar, but word got around among the enlisted men that the members of that gun crew had stew that night.

We had two P-40 pilots with us for a while after their planes were shot down. One was Lieutenant MacDaniels, and the other, I can't remember his name for sure, but I think it was Lieutenant Bryant. He had bright red hair. Both were great guys. The one with the red hair had quite a story to tell.

During a dogfight with two Zero Fighters his engine was shot up and he had to bail out. Knowing how the Japs liked to shoot flyers in their parachutes he didn't open his until the last safe moment. The two Zeros had moved on. Thinking he had it made he looked down at the timbered mountain that would be his landing spot. To his horror, he saw a glittering bunch of spears and waving machetes and realized he was heading right for the camp of the near-naked Igorot mountain people.

He knew well their reputation for chopping up Japs. Back in those days pilots of both sides wore leather flight helmets, the Igorot wouldn't be able to tell where he was from. He was coming down fast, but they were making so much noise they couldn't hear him. In desperation he pulled off his leather helmet and ruffled his red hair in the bright sunlight. Immediately their war chants changed to cheers and shouts of "Americano! Americano!"

They treated him like a long-lost member of the family and prepared a feast in his honor. But the feast wasn't quite what he expected. They took one of their starving dogs and let it gorge on half-cooked rice. Then they tied it in the center of their open area. As they all danced around it they kept beating it with clubs until it was not only dead but also tender. It was then partly roasted over an open fire with all of its innards still inside. When the hair had singed off and the carcass warmed clear through, each person cut off meat from the outside and got a handful of the stomach rice. Being the honored guest, our pilot was given the first helping. When he shared his story, he commented that it could have been worse because he understood that sometimes the Igorot ate people.

Our anti-aircraft Battery G (Globe) was only one of six gun batteries that made up the 60th Coast Artillery (AA) Battalion. The others were Boston (B); Chicago (C), (our mother battery); Denver (D); Flint (F); and Hartford (H). There were also searchlight batteries and machine gun batteries. We were the only 60th gun battery on Bataan. All others remained on Corregidor.

Each gun battery had four three-inch AA guns. They fired shells that were three inches in diameter and around twenty-eight inches long, and they weighed twenty-seven pounds each. They had a twenty-one-second powder train fuse. Each gun had a crew consisting of a gun sergeant, gunner, relay man, elevation man, azimuth man, fuse cutter, and a fuse setter. In addition there were five or six ammunition passers and several backup men to fill in as others were put out of action.

The range section had a range sergeant, director operator, azimuth tracker, elevation tracker, several spotters, two trackers, back-ups, and a height finder operator. The height finder sends height and distance to the director. It records the muzzle velocity, air density, direction of flight, direction of the wind, and speed of the flight, then processes this data and sends it to all guns.

Our officers were Captain Abston, the battery commander; Captain Kwiatkowski, the gunnery officer; and First Lieutenant Peterie, the range officer. All were outstanding officers in every way. We had started with just over a hundred men, and a year after landing, not too many had been killed. By this point several of the Battery G men were badly hurt, some carried shrapnel, and several had lost their hearing in one or both ears. All were suffering from starvation and several also had chills and fever. I was still in as good a shape as any even though my side was festering after the encounter with the sniper.

On one of my next sniper details, I spotted a large flying fruit bat—"flying foxes" I have heard them called. They are monstrous. This one had a body the size of a pigeon and a wingspan of at least four feet. The mountain people considered them a real delicacy. Its big, slow-flopping wings gave the appearance that it wasn't moving very fast even when it was. I decided to follow it to see if it would lead me to a tree of fruit. Both would be a great addition to our watery soup pot.

In no time I had lost sight of it. On turning a bend in the game trail, I came face-to-face with a Filipino man. He probably was only in his thirties, but being so thin and wrinkled he looked much older. I asked him if he had seen the fruit bat.

"Yes!" he said. "You get it for me. My girls are very hungry." I asked him how many children he had. "Oh, they are not my children," he said. "They are my prostitutes that I brought from Manila. You tell your soldiers to come, no charge, just bring food. Very hungry!"

"My soldiers are very hungry too," I told him, "and they are not interested in such things."

"Too bad," he said. "War no good. Japs bring no food either."

"Japs?" I said, raising my voice. "What Japs?"

"Oh they come down every night from those caves over there." He pointed above us. You can see them from here."

We were very close to Mariveles as we talked. He would be safe from the snipers because of his prostitutes, for a while at least, but not me. I made a quick retreat and reported the conversation to Captain Abston. He knew about the Japs in the caves and said that they were going to be shelled by one of our subs if any could get in. If not, the engineers would blast the caves shut with dynamite. That's what they ultimately did.

By the end of March, General Parker's II Corps on the east part of Bataan had been forced back to their very last stand and were digging in for what they knew was coming. The Japs, who had gained control of the railroad, were moving in and setting up their heavy artillery. General Jones's I Corps had been forced back to just north of Mariveles. The four landings the Japs had made in the general area of Mariveles had all been forced back out to sea but at a heavy loss. These landings had been at Longoskawayn Point, Agloloma Point, Quinanan Point, and the entrance to the Salalim River.

Filipino civilians who had swarmed into the area for protection—some twenty-six thousand by report—were being cut down by the heavy shelling the same as our fighting men. The roads were destroyed. The artillery had set the jungle on fire. Death was everywhere. Smoke and dust filled the air and blotted out the sun. Dive bombers worked the area relentlessly. I felt so sorry for those poor civilians. They had no defense. They were victims of a ruthless enemy, and we were no longer of any help to them.

One of the blasts that hit close threw me high into the air. Coming down amid dust and clods I landed on my swollen wound under my left arm. It popped open, letting yellow pus and blood run down my side. This relieved the pressure, and though stinking, made it feel much better. The impact, however, made my splitting headache worse.

I was suffering at that time with the mosquito-borne tropical disease dengue fever, which is sometimes referred to as breakbone fever because every bone in your body burns and you have a bright red rash all over.

It being the dry season, there was plenty of fuel for the roaring fire that was sweeping the forest. The heat developed its own updraft. The smoke was awful. The shelling was awful. The bombing was awful. The chaos was awful. And to top it off, there was an earthquake. It seemed the devil himself was having a heyday. As for Corregidor, on April 1, it received its 116th bombing raid. I have no idea how many we had, but the artillery shelling was worse because you couldn't see them coming.

Fresh enemy shock troops, supported with more tanks, hit II Corps on April 4. The Japs came with bared bayonets and were met by bayonets of our malarial men, who didn't have enough food in their bellies to sustain a small dog. On the west side, I Corps was hit by shelling from the warship just offshore. Dive bombers continued a constant pounding.

The Japs tore a hole in the east line and got in behind. But they were wiped out in toe-to-toe fighting. Jap barges with .75 mm artillery guns hit from the rear flank, but II Corps sank many of them. We lowered our anti-aircraft guns to use as field artillery and blasted the enemy point blank.

New squadrons of Jap dive bombers had been added to the old, and they had begun dropping a new bomb that burst just before hitting the ground, throwing fire and shrapnel at belly height. The end was obvious.

Following is part of a message General Wainwright received from President Roosevelt:

Am keenly aware of the tremendous difficulties under which you are waging your great battle. The physical exhaustion of your troops obviously precludes the possibility of a major counterstroke. ... I have nothing but admiration for your soldierly conduct and your performance of your most difficult mission and have every confidence that whatever decision you may sooner or later be forced to make will be dictated only by the best interest of the country and your magnificent troops.

On April 8, 1942, General Moore ordered Battery G and searchlight Battery E back to Corregidor to stiffen the defense there. The nurses were also to be put on a barge and towed to the Rock. Members of Battery G were ordered to render our artillery guns useless since we were unable to move them.

We broke up the height finder and director and put dynamite in each. The gun crews capped the ends of the three-inch AA guns and filled each breech full of dynamite. The officers sent all of us enlisted men down the mountain to the boat that was waiting for us. They then set off the dynamite with an electric charge. We all had to think about what lay ahead and forget about the attachment we had for the equipment that had served us so well.

There were four tunnels near Mariveles that we had to avoid on our way down the mountainside. Some had contained Japs from one of their not-so-successful landings, but they had been destroyed a few days earlier. All tunnels had been set with high explosives. At least two were exploded as we went down. The air was filled with smoke, dust, and flying debris.

Down at the little harbor boat we were not allowed aboard until Captain Abston arrived and identified his men. Others were turned back. In all there were only around twenty-three hundred people who made it to the Rock, some by boat and some by swimming. Some were washed out to sea. It was sad practically giving a death sentence to those who had to stay and be captured. It was pitch dark except for the flashlight that would be shined in our face to identify each of us.

As we were departing, number four tunnel, where the gasoline was stored, was exploded. It was the biggie of the explosions. Large rocks and parts of human bodies flew through the air. The small boats nearby were sunk with their occupants.

As our little boat headed for Corregidor, I, with a high fever, faded into a coma.

Chapter IV

The Death of Corregidor

The little boat docked in the wee hours of the morning on the north side of Corregidor amid showers of shrapnel from Bataan. Someone was shaking me, but I couldn't seem to get my mind and body synchronized. The weeks of tension and being undernourished had taken their toll.

Someone said, "Hurry! Get to some cover, quick!" Two people—I don't know who—half-carried me off the boat and up a steep bank. I heard someone say, "This is Graham, I think." Another voice said, "We'll take him."

The next thing I remember is that I was in some kind of a cave, and a man was talking to me. He offered me a drink from a canteen. My throat was parched from the fever. I noticed he had the corpsman white-cross armband around his sleeve. Every bone in my body was aching as though a hot poker was being thrust through the marrow of my bones. I was dizzy, and everything kept fading in and out, and I still had that splitting headache.

As the corpsman touched the canteen to my lips, I grabbed it in desperation with both hands, tipped it up, and started gurgling down its contents. He tried to grab it away from me, but I turned my head and kept on drinking. I saw his eyes bug out from fear and horror. He jerked it from my hands. I was going to thank him but fumes came up into my nose, my eyes watered, and I couldn't catch my breath. I struggled, gasping for breath. I was sure I was going to die right then and there. I heard him say, "My God, man! That stuff is half coke syrup and half pure hospital alcohol." I could feel my heart pounding and my blood racing. I passed out.

Some time later—I don't know if it was minutes, hours, or days—someone was trying to wake me up. Talk about a headache! It was as if I had a gigantic jack-o-lantern for a head and someone was inside it beating on a big bass drum. A voice said, "Captain Ames wants you up at Battery C right away. They just lost their director man."

Battery C (Chicago) was on the north slope of Corregidor in full sight of the line-up of Jap artillery that was now assembled along the south beach of Bataan. They'd zeroed in on Battery C and were pounding it unmercifully with .75mm and 105 mm shells. The Battery C AA guns, being at a higher elevation, had difficulty firing back at them.

I was thinking we could run through the heavy underbrush without being seen. I was wrong. There was no underbrush, just burnt snags and shell holes. We leaped from one shell hole to the next. Captain Ames was in the Battery C cave waiting for us. He looked so much older now, but he was still the fine gentleman whom I had known from before, always more concerned about his men than about himself.

There was a bowl of soup waiting for me. It helped my raw stomach. That alcohol should have killed all the bugs that may have been in my digestive system. Captain Ames patiently waited until I had finished my soup and then told me he had several of the Battery G men now, and I should meet with them in their little shell-proof communication shack when the shelling let up. He wanted me to make a list of the articles each might need. With that he slipped out and back to his gun pits. I noticed he had quite a limp as he went out.

One of his men helped me to their communication shack. It was about twelve-by-twelve-foot with a four-inch-thick concrete floor. The double walled sides were of corrugated steel sheeting set about two feet apart. The area between these double walls was filled with sand. The roof was a single layer of corrugated galvanized sheeting. The entire building had been built under a large mango tree that now stood leafless.

Inside was a small, old-style army telephone switchboard that required the operator to wear headphones. The operator had to plug in a line to answer a ring. There was a double-high army bunk bed. At one end of it was a little radio. There was but one chair, which the telephone operator used.

Six of the Battery G men were already there, sitting on the concrete floor, waiting for me. I sat down on the bottom bunk. A little, black shorthaired dog crawled onto my lap. Artillery shells were exploding outside, and we could hear a flight of heavy bombers approaching.

I said a simple prayer, and they bowed their heads, offering up their own. I remember my prayer well. Everything seemed so hopeless, all I had to say was, "Dear Lord, not my will but thine be done." As I said those words, Tokyo Rose was spreading her usual discouraging propaganda over the radio.

We heard a planeload of bombs starting to explode around us. Someone said, "This is it." Psalm 91:11 flashed through my mind: "For he shall give his angels charge over thee." Then it happened. One bomb, with its whizzing sound, came through the roof, dead center.

There was a terrific flash! I heard no sound. Then there was complete darkness.

I felt so relieved. It seemed as though I was floating up. It was a wonderful feeling. I looked down and saw a large hole in the center of the floor. Around it were parts and pieces of the men's bodies. I also saw my body, still sitting there on the bed. The little dog was dead, lying upside down on the radio, which was smoking.

It was more like a vision than reality. I could wriggle like a spirit, but I just couldn't get my lower part free from my body. Everything was so quiet. I saw many others, but at a distance, all were so pleasant and smiling. Strange, but I realized that there was no apparent gender, men or women. All were the same.

Then a dazzling bright ball of light appeared, and a soft voice said, "No, I have something else for you to do."

With that I started drifting back down into my body. I didn't want to go back, but gradually I did. I felt sad when returning to that body. There seemed to be no oxygen in the air. I gasped for breath, but it didn't satisfy. Yellow bomb smoke rolled all around. The four walls had been blown out in all directions. The sheet metal walls were in crumpled ruin. I couldn't see the floor or the other men, or for that matter, even my own body below the waist. I recalled seeing other blast victims with their bowels popped out and wondered if mine were in a similar state.

A wind brought in fresh air and began clearing the smoke. Men from the gun crews were coming in over the rubble. Their lips were moving, but I couldn't hear a word they were saying. I saw the hole in the floor again and the bits of the men. My body was intact but my pants were in shreds. I couldn't move, and I had no feeling in my extremities. They carried me out and back to the cave.

Again I lay in that cave, unable to help those brave Battery C men who were being shelled relentlessly. There were waves after waves of bombers, but the shelling from the artillery was even more dreaded, mainly because there was no telling when they were coming. All of a sudden they were just there, leaving no time to take cover.

Captain Ames and others, including First Sergeant Beeman, kept checking on me. My hearing started to come back in one ear. Then word came that Captain Abston had assembled enough equipment to start up Battery G again. It was now going to be on the very top of Corregidor, right in the center of the golf course, in the center of the island, "The Bull's Eye."

This made some sense, because the golf course was relatively flat. It would be much harder for the artillery to hit with their flat-shooting artillery shells. As for bombers, well they just dumped their bombs everywhere anyway. Besides, we would be able to see the bombers coming, shoot back, and then take cover. The dive bombers were something else.

Archie, a little monkey mascot, had been raised in one of the batteries and was a bit spoiled. He was a funny little guy who was always up to some kind of mischief. I remembered him from peacetime. He would jump onto a guy's shoulder—it could be anyone—pull off the guy's cap, and search through his hair. I don't know if he was looking for fleas or if it was just a grooming instinct.

As I was to rejoin Battery G, the C Battery C cook told me to drop by their dug-out kitchen. He said he had made me a corn fritter and had put it in a big iron pot that had a big heavy lid on it. When I slid down into the dimly lighted kitchen, I spotted the pot immediately, but something didn't seem right. I was sure the lid moved. There was a lot of earth shaking from all of the shelling, but the movement I saw hadn't been caused by the shelling.

I stood there for a moment. Then the lid slowly lifted a crack. Two little beady black eyes peeked out. Yes, it was Archie! When I called his name, he threw the lid back, let out a terrified scream, and leaped onto my back. In his mouth was what was left of my corn fritter. He was in such a state of shell shock that I couldn't get him quieted down. Finally he jumped back into the pot and pulled the big lid back over him.

When I arrived at our new site, the men had already dug shallow trenches connecting all gun pits, and all the sand bagging had been done. They were ready to orient and synchronize our three-inch AA guns. That night amid shelling we oriented all guns, the height finder, and the director on one big bright star. The gunners placed cross hairs—small strings—on the end of each of the AA guns and boresighted them in. We were so intent on accuracy that several, myself included, got hit with shrapnel in our backs. Mine was so deep that it stayed in for several weeks, until it finally festered out later in prison camp.

With the increase of those of us from Bataan, Corregidor was bulging with people. This made the already short supply of ammunition, food, and water even more critical. The dry season in the Philippines runs from November to June, and it was April. Water had to be rationed. We were given a canteenful morning and evening after drawing our chow. In addition, we got a canteen cupful once a day for washing. About all we could do with that small amount was to wet a rag and wipe off the sweat and dirt, but most of us just drank it. The intense shelling and bombing by now had eliminated all vegetation, leaving the surface of the Rock resembling the crater-marked surface of the moon.

The negligible chow had to be served after dark and before daylight to keep the enemy observation planes from seeing the lineup of men. By this point, food was usually a gruel of cracked grain or rice, or a combination of both. Our battery G of the 60th Anti-Aircraft was served down the hill a short distance away in the big concrete mortar pits of the 59th Coast Artillery's Battery Geary. We could get there and back by running through the zigzag trenches that connected our two positions.

Battery Geary was in a location that was hard to hit from Bataan, and for a while it played a heavy toll on the enemy. It was by far the most effective defense we had at that time. It had two big concrete gun pits, each with four twelve-inch mortars. They fired 670-pound shells. These shells had to be moved to the mortars on special carts that were equipped with conveyer belts. Big bags of explosive powder were slid in behind. When they fired, it sounded like a freight train taking off into the sky.

An ammunition storage room was located between the two pits. It was protected by thick walls, a concrete ceiling, and heavy reinforced steel doors. These doors faced north, in the direction of our position. They were kept closed except when loading.

One time I watched the gun crew load. The size of the projectiles and the proficiency of the crew were so impressive that I stood there with my mouth open. After everyone disappeared, a loud buzz sounded. I wondered what that was for. Someone yelled, "Get the hell out of there or you'll be flattened against that concrete wall from the concussion!" I made a flying leap up and over the concrete wall just in time. There was a mighty bang and a roar as four of the 670-pound projectiles raced off into the sky.

Japan thought they could take the entire Philippines in less than two months. It now had been more than five months so the pressure was really being put on their leaders. They added more heavy bombers and increased the number of missions for them to fly. We could just about tell what area they were going to bomb next because it would be worked over by their dive bombers first in hopes of knocking out our anti-aircraft guns or at least driving us into our foxholes. Their bombs would then be dropped, followed by heavy shelling from their artillery to keep us from firing back.

But as the dive bombers moved out, we jumped back to our guns and got off a round or two, and then hit the dirt again before the artillery shells came in. Their observation plane, however, soon caught on to our strategy, and they tightened the intervals, which caused us more casualties. By this point every one of us had been wounded more than once. It was anyone's guess as to when his number would come up. There was no way to remove the dead and no place to put them if there had been. It was all very hard on our nerves.

At times some dive bombers zipped in with machine guns blazing, dropped their bombs, and got out again while the bombs from the big planes were still on their way down.

Day after day the shelling and bombing continued. One day would slide into the next, but no one was concerned as to what day it was. Each additional day we could hold out would be one more day for our country to build up a return force. There was no way *we* could be saved. Somewhere during this time I had my twenty-second birthday, and I wasn't even aware of it.

There was no place on the bleak golf course that was safe. We all were reconciled to the fact that if we got hit, we just got hit. If we lived, we could fight another day.

I was so completely exhausted one day that I told those in the range section that I was going to take my old wool blanket and drop down on the ground out in the open by a snag of a tree and sleep, which I did. Dirt and debris showered over me, but I managed to sleep.

One of our men shook me and said that the captain wanted us to take the height finder down to the Malinta Tunnel and exchange it for a repaired one. Ours had some broken mirrors in it from shrapnel. I rolled out, leaving my blanket there, and gave them a hand.

It was pitch dark except for the shell bursts all around. Somehow—by luck, the use of an old truck, and a man a walking ahead with a flashlight, guiding us around shell and bomb holes—we made it down the Geary-Malinta Hill road and back.

Leaving the range section crew to set up the repaired height finder, I headed back to where my blanket had been. It wasn't there. In its place, heading down the hill to the south, was a deep groove. I slipped down into it on my hands and knees and followed it in the dark for about thirty feet, and there found my blanket pierced with a 155 mm Jap dud and partly buried in the base of an old uprooted snag of a tree. I tried to pull the blanket out, but it wasn't possible. I was just glad I hadn't been sleeping in it.

On another day, either a bomb or a shell exploded inside one of the gun pits, killing some of the gun crew and also closing the nearby trench where three of the relief gunners were crouched. They were completely buried, and we could hear their muffled yells for help. Many shovels, bare hands, and tin hats dug frantically to get them out before they suffocated. We made it. Their tin hats had given them just enough air space to permit them to keep re-breathing the dusty air. As we pulled them out they were a dirty, pitiful sight. They were tough, though, and still full of fight. I remember one of them saying, "Which one of you was the SOB who was standing on my back?" It was really just the weight of the dirt on him.

A few days later, after a hit to one of the AA guns put it out of action, part of its crew slipped down over the bank and onto the south shore road to wait until repairs were made. It was considered to be the safest place we had. There was a high vertical bank on the north side and an abrupt drop off on the south. The crew had spread their blankets out on the narrow road. There was no longer shade anywhere. Bombing and shelling by now was so constant and commonplace it was practically ignored. They busied themselves patching up wounds with makeshift bandages and trying to give comfort and encouragement to each other.

Suddenly a bomb made a direct hit right in the center of them. "There has been a direct hit on the guys on the road!" someone yelled. The others and I raced to the edge and down the bank. What a mess met our eyes! Some were still alive.

One of my best friends recognized me and raised up and started running toward me with arms outstretched. He said, "Graham, help me!" His intestines were hanging out and he was stepping on them and pulling them out as he came. He died in my arms. One man was walking around with only part of a head. He walked directly into the north bank then fell over backwards, dead. Those of us left are certainly not heroes; we are just the ones who didn't die.

On April the 28, the enemy added 240 mm guns to their line of artillery on Bataan. Shells from these weigh over four hundred pounds each. When these big guns were added to their line, we knew our remaining days were few. It was estimated that they had at least five hundred artillery guns lined up and working us over from the Bataan side alone. That number didn't include all of those that were firing from the south.

April 29 was Emperor Hirohito's birthday. We knew that they wanted Corregidor for his birthday present, and we were determined that he wouldn't get it. More than ten thousand artillery shells landed on us that day. We stayed put, hoping that one didn't join us in our foxhole. The air was so full of shrapnel, to dodge it was like trying to dodge hail in a hailstorm. Casualties skyrocketed.

During that night, a Philippine Army liaison plane somehow made it in, holding low to the water, and back out again with some of the key people on board. General Wainwright refused to leave his men. Three war correspondents made it out on the plane: Clark Lee, Dean Schedler, and Frank Hewlett. They took the last brutal details of what was happening back to the States.

On April 30 a direct hit on one of our guns killed eleven of the crew and badly wounded a dozen more. The morale of our battery remained amazingly good considering our horrific losses and injuries. All of us were geared to die fighting, and that helped.

One dark morning in the chow line down at Battery Geary, I heard one of the men ahead of me say, "I think this is May Day. May Day! May Day!" Then a sullen voice from farther back in the line replied, "What year?" That told a lot about how we all felt.

By this point all of the Battery C AA guns had been completely destroyed. Some of their three-inch mechanically fused ammunition had been brought over to us, and we were grateful for them. This was the start of the five days of the heaviest concentration of bombing and shelling that the Rock ever received.

The next day, May 2, the Japs concentrated their fire on us because our battery and Battery Geary were still active. For five full hours they hit us at the rate of twelve shells per minute, thirty-six hundred rounds by actual count. We were unable to man our guns to even fire back one round during that entire period. Their observation planes circled overhead, directing their fire.

They walked their fire back and forth over us. Battery Geary had previously lost the four twelve-inch mortars in their A pit. Now the shelling was chipping away the heavy concrete around their B pit. Also the heavy steel doors of the ammunition magazine were giving away.

A little after 4 p.m. a 240 mm shell crashed through the steel doors and exploded inside the ammunition magazine. Sixteen hundred of the sixty-two-pound fully charged powder charges exploded. The blast was so great that it shook the entire Rock as if there were an earthquake. The twelve-inch mortars, which weighed thirteen tons each, were ripped from their concrete bases and scattered like leaves. One landed nose down by us on the golf course, 150 yards from its base. A huge section of concrete, some thirteen-feet thick, landed even farther, completely clearing our position. It landed right where my blanket had been before it had been swept up by that dud.

After this blast there was a pause in the shelling. I heard one of our officers say, "They are getting a little rough aren't they?" He was wiping blood from his face but grinning.

On May 3, our Battery Globe was still firing. That night a submarine, *The Spearfish*, made it in and out again, taking twenty-five people, including thirteen women. How it made it was a miracle.

As our defense batteries were destroyed one after another, the men who were still alive became part of the beach defense group to help turn back an invasion in one last stand. As this group grew, it included men from the Coast Guard, air force, navy, marines, the Philippine

Scouts and Army, the constabulary, office workers, medics, and civilians. They took whatever weapons were available to them. Some had never fired a weapon before and had no infantry training. The Fourth Marines, now few in number, were the main part of this put-together defense group.

The obvious landing place for the enemy's invasion was the ten thousand feet of the north shoreline on the eastern end of the island, the tail of Corregidor. There were no steep rock banks there, just a flat beach. Our defense was organized with this in mind. If their initial landing could maintain a foothold, thousands more would follow. As it soon turned out, that is where the Japs hit—by the thousands.

Just to the west of this area was a low ridge called the Hogback. Our 60th AA Battery Denver was stationed there and still active. Just to the west of this ridge was Malinta Tunnel, the nerve center of our whole operation. In it was the command center and the hospital, which was filled with the wounded.

On May 4, some sixteen thousand shells (as reported later by Japan) rained down on Corregidor. By the end of that day nearly all of our artillery had been blasted out of action. The Rock's great guns were silent. Empty shell casings littered the area. All vegetation, buildings, roads, gun emplacements, and even the little railroad had been destroyed. Men slid from crater to crater, trying to out-guess where the next explosion would be. All communication lines, electric lines, and water lines had also been destroyed. Millions of big blowflies swarmed over the dead bodies.

All day on May 5, the shelling was concentrated on the eastern part of the island. Our area, the high ground, had been beat to pulverized rock. Our men, mainly artillerymen, organized into a smaller reserve beach defense group to back up the first group. I was in this group. We armed ourselves with pistols, a rifle, ammunition, and as many hand grenades as we could carry.

We formed into two single-line columns and walked silently down the south shore road. We moved down through the smoldering Middleside area, our once pleasant peacetime home, down through the Bottomside section, where once stood native fruit stands operated by Filipino civilians, then around the south side of Malinta Hill to the east end of the Malinta Tunnel. Men from headquarters met us there and briefed us on conditions on the east end of the island. The enemy invasion was expected to start at any time.

How many of our original beach defense were still alive was unknown to headquarters. Their guess was that most were now dead. We also were informed that several barges full of enemy shock troops were waiting just off shore for orders to start their invasion. They would get the go-ahead as soon as their shelling stopped. Our assignment was to join the men at the water's edge. I and several other men joined forces to take North Point. It was pitch dark as we started, except for the flashing light from the exploding shells.

As we crossed Hogback, several enemy flares popped off above. Their light reflected downward from the low-hanging cloud of smoke and gave us a quick look at the area ahead. As the light faded we made a mad dash for our beach destination. The man at my left took a bullet or a chunk of shrapnel in the chest and fell. I heard the wind go out of him, so I kept on going. I lost track of the man on my right.

The distance to the beach seemed much farther than it had looked. Finally I heard the lapping of the water just ahead. Several of the first beach defense men were lying there. I dropped in between two of them just as the Japs launched several incendiary bombs. They were not close, but they lit up the area a little. I could see the barges full of Japs not far out.

  I also saw the two men I had crawled between. They were marines, and they were dead and had been for some time. Their bodies were puffed up and had turned black from the tropical heat. I wriggled in close between the two and rested my rifle across the swollen chest of the one on my right and softly said to him, "Just one more job for you to do old friend: protect me from their fire."

Soon, as predicted, the shelling stopped. It was about 11 p.m. The moon was just starting to show a little light in the eastern sky when I heard the chains rattle on the barges as they let down the gates so the troops could come ashore. The air filled with the shouts of crazed, hopped-up Japs shouting "*Bonzai!*" and other unfamiliar screams. Guns opened up and bullets sung like I had never heard before. Bataan had been bad, but we had never faced a multitude like this.

I shot point blank into the advancing hoard. I fired all of my rifle ammunition, then all of my pistol ammunition. I pulled the pins on my hand grenades, one by one, and threw them among the advancing troops.

Behind those who fell came more. They dropped down as they reached the land and started crawling in.

By this time my heart was pounding so fast and loud that I was sure they could hear it above all the commotion. I tried to roll my dead Marine protector over to get his rifle but he was too squishy. Bullets or shrapnel had opened up his far side and a terrible odor was coming out. I jerked his rifle free and tried to work the bolt, but it was jammed with sand and wouldn't budge.

There was movement all around me. Our machine gun that had been firing just a few feet to my right was now silent. I heard Jap grunts and low voices ahead of me, behind me, and on both sides. The moon was by this point high enough to shed a little light. On the other side of my dead marine friend to my left was a man who was very much alive. He was facing inland. As he raised his head to look around, I saw that he was a Jap. I slipped the bayonet from my rifle, raised up on my knees, and brought it down, full force, into his back. I added my full weight to force it deeper. That bayonet was my last defense weapon.

I could see hundreds of dead Japs in orange life jackets floating in the water. I could also see many crabs crawling over the beach and feeding on the dead bodies. The bay was full of sharks, so I'm sure they were having a feast too.

For the first time a strange fear hit me. What could I do? I was lying among dead Americans and living Japs. Then it occurred to me that the situation was really in *my* favor. All I had to do was to run right through the middle of them. They wouldn't fire at each other.

I ran as hard as I could run, right across the backs of the dead and the living. Back in my high school days I had set a school record for the hundred-yard dash, but this run was even faster. I doubt that I even took a breath until I reached the Hogback.

I tumbled into a pit with some other Americans. When I caught my breath I gasped, "Thank God I made it."

"No you haven't," one of the guys said. "We are surrounded by Japs, they are between us and Malinta Tunnel."

"No problem," I gasped. "I just found out that I can out-run any bullet," and with that I took off again as fast as my legs could carry me. I hit right in between two Japs in my path, knocking them both over, and on I went.

At the east entrance to the Malinta Tunnel some officers were giving orders. They asked me what outfit I was from. I told them Globe. A full colonel said, "Your Captain Abston wants you guys to join him up at your old gun position on the golf course. He has some of your AA guns back in operation." I immediately took off.

I was so tired by that point that I had to stop every little bit. The climb up the rockslide, where the Golden Stairs had been, seemed much steeper now. My drive was fading. Others of our battery were heading back too. Some at the site hadn't gone down at all.

I joined the crew, and we got in some good shooting. The Jap planes were flying low and not expecting our fire. We knocked down two for sure and turned off several others before we were knocked out again.

Colonel Breitung and several other officers were discussing what to do. It was now the morning of May 6,

1942. They were saying that General Wainwright had decided that he would order a surrender to save the sick and wounded in the hospital from being massacred. President Roosevelt had given him that ultimatum. A white flag would be raised at noon to replace the Stars and Stripes. This would exemplify the death of Corregidor.

As I heard that we were going to surrender, tears started flowing down my cheeks and a lump swelled in my throat. All terrible things seemed to have a way of getting worse. Others were crying as well. We were so dehydrated that I have no idea how we could cry.

We had lost Bataan, and now we were going to lose Corregidor? The sad fact was that without air and naval power and without food, ammunition, and weapons there was no way that we could hold back a superpower enemy. We still had the will to fight, but the choice was no longer ours. If only we had something to fight with.

Defeat is a hard pill to swallow. Weird logic pops into one's mind at a time like this. I wondered if it would take some of their fighting men away from their front line to guard us prisoners. We would be more of a problem to them alive than dead. I wondered how would my mother and father take it. And I wondered what that friendly old bum on the docks in San Francisco meant the night of my departure when he said, "I'll be with you in spirit."

We were told to take off individually because of the shelling and to regroup at the old Battery Wheeler site. There we were to clean up, put on the clean uniforms we would find there, shave, fill a canteen with water, and assemble again by the flag pole for the march down to meet our captors. Colonel Breitung said, "I'm ordering you to go down, but I'm staying here. They're going to have to come up and get me."

We destroyed our guns and ammunition as ordered and packed a bag of items usable in prison camp. Then we headed down to Middleside, the grouping area.

We had lost the battle, but we had won time, which was so badly needed for the folks back home. The crippling blow the Japs had made on Pearl Harbor before declaring war had severely weakened our Pacific navy and air force. Our Atlantic forces were already committed to assisting Great Britain in its war with Germany. Japan, through treachery and deceit, had gained control of the Pacific with their sights on Australia.

Malaya had fallen into Japanese hands on January 31, 1942, and Singapore was taken on February 15 of the same year. But Bataan and Corregidor had held long enough, even just these few months, to deprive Japan the use of Manila Bay and the harbor that they so badly needed as a hub for their expanding empire. Also, this had given the U.S. time to build up its Pacific fleet and air power.

It's hard to recall the details of what went on at Middleside, but there was much confusion. Men were milling around like zombies, and Jap shells were still falling on us. They seemed intent on killing as many of us as they could before imprisoning us, and they were doing a good job of it.

An American officer came running into our group ahead of a small group of Japanese officers. "Clear the way!" he yelled. "Don't touch them! Give them room."

One of the Jap officers could speak a little English. He interpreted the screaming of a higher-ranking Jap officer. We were to get into groups and march down through Bottomside and on into the 92nd garage parking area.

As we formed into groups, little bandy-legged Jap enlisted men poked us with bayonets, hit, and shoved us, screaming, "*Kudasai! Kudasai!*" and "*Hyakka! Hyakka!*" Some of our men were killed on the spot because they were not sure what they were supposed to do. Yes, things were still getting worse. The evils of hell have no limits. How naive I had been back in Fort Riley, Kansas, when I sought a challenge and said, "I want a transfer to where there will be some action."

The 60th men grouped together. We were formed into columns of four, a hundred men to a group. Captain Abston and I were at the head of one group, he on the right and I on his left. As we marched through Bottomside, a Jap photographer took pictures of us. One of these pictures became well publicized. However, it was erroneously captioned as the "Captives of Bataan," while in reality, it was taken right there at Bottomside.

As we were prodded along, Jap enlisted men stripped us of rings, watches, pens, and anything else that caught their eye. I slipped my graduation ring into my mouth, so they didn't get it at that time.

We were herded into the parking lot of the 92nd garage, an area about the size of two city blocks, and held there in the blistering tropical sun for several days without food or water. The Corregidor water supply had been destroyed. By evening of the first day there were so many men crowded into the area that there was hardly room to sit. Any food or water had to be guarded. Many of our hungry and thirsty men became almost uncivilized in their attempt to survive. Food and water were stolen in the dark of night.

It was estimated that there were around sixteen thousand of us in this small area. There were no toilets, and trench toilets could not be dug because of the concrete. Flies multiplied rapidly and dysentery spread.

Groups quickly formed for protection. Many of the weak and old died. The amputees and severely wounded were removed, and we never saw them again. If the Japs thought they would be of no value as slave laborers, they were probably killed.

Some water was eventually discovered under the plank-covered grease pits, and chlorine was somehow obtained from the Japs. The volume was calculated and it was dumped into the stinking water. The mixture was stirred up, and we lined up and filled our canteens. The taste was terrible, but the water was a lifesaver for many of us.

One of the Jap officers in charge of us was an interpreter who spoke very good English. He was a good six feet tall and somewhat polite, unlike the others, who seemed more animal-like. He had called for some of us to help bring boxes of Corregidor supplies and food out of Malinta Tunnel. I volunteered, thinking that I could get something to eat, but no luck. With every carton that I carried there was a Jap guard at my side yelling, "Speedo!" and pushing and hitting me.

The boxes I carried contained canned peas. I stacked these boxes on the docks, and other prisoners loaded them onto a boat. The path I had to go down went right by a pitful of Japanese shock troops. These were dirty, mean, unshaven savages. Other Jap soldiers had machine guns trained on them to keep them under control. As I passed they were receiving rations of raw ground meat. My guard walked between me and them with fixed bayonet pointing at them. He watched them closely. He seemed to be afraid of them.

When I got a chance to talk to the Jap interpreter again I asked him about the men and why there were machine guns pointed at them. He told me that they were very dangerous special shock troop marines, and they got a ration of raw meat after every invasion. They would be moved out very soon. He said that they had been little boys who had no parents, and the army raised them. They had no schooling and were only taught how to kill.

The blistering tropical sun beat down and reflected back up from the paving, making the area feel like an oven. Men were packed so closely together that only those on the outer perimeter of the crowd could feel a breeze. Heat blisters and heat strokes added to the misery. There was no shade. Some groups put up blankets and shelter-halves, but quite a few still died.

Burial details were sent out to bury the dead Americans and Filipinos. The dead Japs had to be stacked and burned. An arm was cut off of each to be sent home to his family to be cremated and honored in the family's shrine.

Flies swarmed over the dead bodies, and maggots tumbled out as we lifted and carried them. Some of the dead had swollen so much that buttons had popped off their uniforms. The stench was sickening. The Jap guards wore masks over their noses but we had none. Our chaplains tried to make up casualty lists, but they were only permitted to give a quick prayer over each. In two days the job was pretty well completed.

After a few days of hunger and thirst, the Japs let some men carry a few boxes of food out of Malinta Tunnel to feed our thousands. The food was delivered to our officers for distribution. They did the best that they could distributing it, but by that point discipline had broken down. Heat, pain, anger, hunger, thirst, and despair changed men, bringing out the worst in some and the best in others.

Chapter V

The Victory March

We were confined in this 92nd garage area for around two weeks. I remember that rain relieved the heat for a short time, and it allowed us to clean our bodies a bit. We were also able to catch some of the rainwater with the shelter-halves for drinking.

Then came the day that we were ordered to move out. All kinds of rumors circulated. They formed us in groups of one hundred. With much screaming and yelling, they marched us the short distance to the South Docks. Some of the very weak were jerked out of line, shoved, beaten, and led off. That was the last we ever saw of them.

Three small ships were anchored at the docks. With more screaming and yelling, we were forced to climb up the side of a ship about eighteen feet on a sort of coarse net, carrying our possessions with us. I carried my duffel bag, containing an extra pair of shoes, a change of clothes, my canteen and mess kit, and a pint bottle of seven percent iodine. I didn't have any food or water.

As I reached the top of the ship's side, a Jap sailor grabbed my bag from me and threw it into a pile of other bags, breaking the iodine bottle and staining my clothes. He jerked my head down, causing me to land on my head on the deck, and then kicked me in the face.

This ship had been used to transport horses. The hold that we were forced into was littered with at least a half-foot of horse manure and urine-soaked straw. They crowded more and more of us in until we were packed tight. We spent the night like that. I thought how horses could sleep standing up because they can lock up their stifles, but we're not made that way. The only good thing was that no one complained about not having any toilet—we were standing in one.

The next morning the ships pulled anchor and chugged along for about an hour and a half. They had crossed the bay to the shore south of the city of Manila. The ships anchored some distance from shore. We were ordered out and over the side to barges that had pulled up alongside the ships. We climbed down the rope nets and were packed into the barges. Our bags were thrown down at us. I had no trouble spotting mine because of the iodine stains.

These barges headed for shore but stopped short. They checked the depth and if it was less than eight feet, the barge was backed to that depth. We were then ordered over the side with our bags and motioned to swim for shore. I was glad that my bag was only about one-third full. It stayed afloat until I could touch bottom with my feet. Some of the bags, however, went right to the bottom and couldn't be retrieved. The Japs really enjoyed watching the sinking bags. The barges could have been driven right up to the shoreline, but making us swim in was one more way to humiliate us.

We went ashore, soaking wet, and were hit with clubs that were about five feet long and made of bamboo or two-by-two-inch boards. These were swung with full force. Some of the men were knocked unconscious. These Japs seemed to be practicing for the baseball season. They lined us up in groups of one hundred, four abreast, for their victory march through the capital city of Manila. We began at the south end of Dewey Boulevard.

This march, I'm sure, was intended to impress the civilian population with Japan's power and great victory. Each group began marching at a fast pace set by a Jap officer on horseback. Little screaming guards ran along beside us, hitting and yelling, "Speedo!" I carried my bag over my back to ward off the blows, but I received several hard whacks on the top of my head. We later nicknamed these clubs "vitamin sticks."

After about half a mile we encountered crowds of Filipinos lining the streets. Among them were wives and children of some of the men. The Japs were really surprised, however, when the crowd showed their compassion by crying and throwing candy, cigarettes, and food to us. Cries of "Long live MacArthur!" could be heard all along the way. Flashes of the two-finger V sign for victory could be seen everywhere. All of this show of compassion tended to infuriate the guards even more.

A very pregnant lady was dipping out water from a jar. As I passed her, she handed me a dipperful. I thanked her, but before I could get the dipper to my lips a guard knocked it from my hand. Then he ran his bayonet clear through her and her unborn baby. She fell to the ground, screaming. The guard placed his foot on her stomach and jerked out his bayonet, and then proceeded on, looking for others. As the expression of sympathy for us grew louder, the guards started running into the crowd, swinging their clubs and hitting everyone they could.

The Filipinos lining the street were shocked and horrified at the brutality and the vicious, evil acts of these Japs. Any of the Filipinos who may have thought they would be well treated certainly had a change of mind with this demonstration. We saw a young man beheaded. Several people had to run for their lives to avoid one sword-swinging Jap. The difference between these two cultures were obvious: the Filipinos were easygoing and friendly, and the Japanese were cruel.

Some of our weakest could not keep up with the fast pace and fell. They were never seen again, no doubt killed by the guards. Many of us had received no food or water for several days, and the only things that kept us going were prayer and determination.

It was nearly dark as we entered the gates to the old and empty Bilibid Prison. Most of us dropped to the ground and just lay there. I was so tired and thirsty and hungry that I began to tremble. The calves of my legs knotted up, and I ached in every joint and muscle. As miserable as I was, however, there was the comforting thought that I had at least made it that far. That was more than could be said for so many. The moans and groans of the bruised and depressed Americans were the only sounds. The Filipino soldiers had been separated from us earlier.

    Around ten that night, the Japs finally gave us food. They brought in several five-gallon cans of steamed rice and some weak tea. We quietly lined up and drew our ration. I tried to eat mine slowly, but I began gulping it down. I wound up with some terrible stomach cramps. I laid down on my back in the dirt and looked up at the star-studded sky and the guards with their rifles walking the high prison walls above us and wondered if the folks back home had any idea what was happening to us. I hoped that they didn't, but I hoped God was watching.

Chapter VI

Cabanatuan

I dreamed I was being kicked and yelled at by a Jap guard. As I woke I found that it wasn't just a dream; I really was being kicked by one. Many of our fellows were already lining up. It was still as dark as pitch except for the prison lights. We again lined up in four columns with one hundred to a group, counted and recounted, and then marched out of the big iron gates of Bilibid Prison. We had no idea where we were going or how the war was going. For all we knew we were being marched out to be executed. We stumbled along for what seemed like miles. (Later I found out that it was only about two miles.) They stopped us by a railroad track.

The sun was coming up, and we could tell that it was going to be a scorcher of a day. There were several small boxcars on the railroad track. They were like the old French Forty and Eight boxcars of WWI, designed to hold forty men or eight horses. They were about eight feet wide and thirty-three feet long with seven-foot ceilings.

The Japs forced a group of one hundred men into each of these cars, and then with yelling, hitting, and poking with bayonets, they forced in up to fifteen more. We were packed so tightly that it was hard to draw a full breath. The doors were slid shut and locked. All ventilation holes had been boarded up. The cars just sat there. The sun outside rose, as did the temperature inside. Oxygen was depleting rapidly, and we were breathing each other's breath over and over again. We yelled and pounded on the sides and on the door and called for air but got no response. Men started fainting, but they couldn't fall. Our body heat raised the temperature higher than that outside. Our bodies were slimy from sweat and dehydrating on the inside.

The brain plays cruel tricks on one when under desperate situations. Some men became raving maniacs. Some suffocated to death. Those with severe cases of dysentery couldn't control their bowels and defecated on themselves and those behind them. The heat, the stench, the yelling, the swearing, the praying, and the dying made the experience a real hell that I will never forget.

Finally the train pulled out. After several hours it stopped. The doors were unlocked and pulled open to let in air. No one was allowed to get out. We could not even send out the dead. We were able to shift around just enough so that some of the dead went down on the floor.

We stood on them. It reminded me of back home when we had a brooder full of little chickens and how on a cold night they would crowd together to keep warm. In the morning we would find some standing on those that had died. After about ten minutes of fresh air the doors were closed and locked, and we were on our way again.

The train pulled into a station midafternoon, and we were ordered out. We were so weak and numb that we could hardly move. The guards yelled and beat us into line and counted us. In our group there were between sixty and seventy of us left. The number sixty-two sticks in my mind, but I'm not sure if it's correct. The Jap in charge of our car counted the dead in the car and seemed real pleased that so many had died. He was laughing at how weak the Americans were. That is the first time I heard the expression *Takusan beyoke*, which I learned later meant "very sick."

We were marched a short distance to an enclosed schoolyard where we spent the night on the ground. There was only one water faucet. We lined up and took turns filling our water containers. That water was cool and wonderful. I knew that in our condition one shouldn't drink too much but I downed a full canteen anyway, and refilled it. It didn't hurt me a bit. At dusk the Japanese gave each of us a rice ball that was about the size of a softball. I ate all of mine because I knew that if I saved any it would be stolen as I slept.

It was the first good night's sleep I'd had since the first bombing raid on Hawaii at the start of WWII. Now there were no bombs or shells or flying bugs or creeping reptiles, and I had food and water in my belly. I stretched out at full length on the cool ground and slept.

At dawn we were lined up again and counted. Some had died during the night. Since the guards didn't get the same count as the night before they said we would get no breakfast. We were marched off, but at least we had full canteens. This schoolyard was somewhere near the town of Cabanatuan.

The sun rose. The day turned hot. The guards weren't too bad at the start. They would walk us a distance then call out, "*Yosume!*" which means "rest." They would then give us a short rest. As the day wore on and became hotter, they became mean again. We were so tired, and our muscles ached and were knotted. Our empty stomachs cramped. Our eyes became blurry, and our minds sputtered off and on like a balky engine about

out of gas. This caused us to stagger. Some who fell could not get back up, and we were too weak to help each other. Some, I'm sure, went down in despair, thinking that it just wasn't worth the price they had to pay. They were killed. The Japs really seemed to enjoy this bayoneting and beating. It seemed to give them a great sense of superiority. They hated Americans with a passion.

    Around noon, we stumbled by a fenced Philippine military training camp that we later learned would be named Cabanatuan Prison Camp Number One. At first sight of the long bamboo barracks, we thought we were nearing our destination. But that wasn't so. The guards yelled and prodded us along.

    By midafternoon we passed a second Philippine training camp. It would be known as Camp Number Two. The guards stopped us in front of it. They seemed confused as to whether we were to be confined at this camp or farther down the road. They finally got it straightened out, and we were marched on. We arrived at Camp Number Three late in the afternoon.

We were stopped on the road just outside the main gate and ordered to dump out our bags and pockets and lay everything we had on the ground in front of us. They screamed that anyone hiding anything from them would be severely punished. We knew what that meant—death.

One man three rows ahead of me had two canteens. One had been full of water. In the other he had stuffed American hundred dollar bills. He was burning up with fever and was offering a hundred dollars for a drink of water. No one was interested. He then pulled out a hundred dollar bill to show that he really had the money and meant it. A guard saw this and jerked him out of line and started beating him. Several guards joined in, and they beat him for a while. Then two of the guards stabbed him repeatedly with their bayonets. He screamed for several minutes before he finally died.

Guards then came through our ranks and checked every canteen. They didn't find any more money in our group, but they made us leave everything on the road and marched us into the camp with nothing but the clothes we had on our backs.

Camp Number Three apparently had not been completed before the start of the war. There was only one working water faucet for our section. The Japs sent in all of the canteens. I didn't get my old one back but got one that was even better—it had a canteen cup with it. All survivors lined up at the water faucet to fill from the slow trickle. I filled both my canteen and the cup.

There were several thousand prisoners in the camp. It was big. The Filipinos were grouped in one area. They were treated much worse than we were. We were assigned to open-air bamboo barracks. These were about sixty feet long and twenty feet wide and made of native vegetation: The framework was constructed of bamboo poles. The sides were made of woven reeds. The roofs were of thatched banana leaves. Strings of rattan held things together. There were no nails or wire or metal of any kind.

Each building had a four-foot-wide catwalk down the center, the full length of the barracks. Upper and lower sleeping bays were on each side of the catwalk. These bays also ran the full length of the barracks. All flooring was of split bamboo spaced about a half-inch apart. Windows were of woven reeds and rattan. They also ran full length of the building. Each individual window was held at the top with rattan and could be propped open at the bottom. Air circulated freely and gave a cooling effect even at the hottest part of the day. These well-built buildings exhibited real Filipino craftsmanship.

    The Japs wanted some of the buildings moved to a new location. About fifty prisoners were assigned to move them. Poles were slid under the buildings, and we were ordered to lift and carry. Some men were so weak that they fell, and then they were beaten until they were back on their feet. Those standing had to hold up the building until these were back up and on their pole. Humane people wouldn't even force a horse to work under those conditions, but these Japs had no respect for life.

Hatred constantly burned within me. My only relief was my determination to survive so that should the opportunity ever present itself, I could get my revenge. That rage burned within me like a smoldering volcano.

Each of the barracks held two hundred men. There must have been several hundred buildings. Ten buildings made up a group. Each group had a kitchen. Each kitchen had a couple of big, round-bottom iron pots. One was for cooking rice and one was for soup. These pots were suspended on three legs made of cinder blocks and adobe clay. Under guard supervision, we had details go out and cut wood for the fires. Americans operated the kitchens: one officer and several enlisted men. These cooks could be distinguished from the rest of us because none of them were thin. I was down to less than a 100 pounds at that time. My peacetime weight had been 164 pounds.

Each kitchen was issued so many grams of rice per man per area, but this amount varied according to the mood of the Japs in charge at the time. When the rice was nearly cooked, the fire would be pulled out from under it, and a burlap-covered wooden lid would be placed on top to let the rice steam until tender.

The soup was mostly boiled greens of some kind: Often tops from comote vines (a Philippine sweet potato), sometimes small plants thinned from vegetable rows, including roots and all, and at times just weeds. On rare occasions there would be a few cubes of meat per pot or a few small, smelly dried fish. We were so starved for protein that whoever got one of these could easily trade it for a half ration of rice. There was a short time when we even received some black beans, but that didn't last long. Each man got one dip of watery soup. The sick received a smaller dip than those who could work. Officers were housed separately from enlisted men and fared somewhat better, and they didn't have to work.

The Jap guards were running through camp, chasing everyone out of the barracks and yelling for us to line up at the main gate. As we stood at the fence at attention, a detail of Japs came into view, bringing up an American soldier. They had his hands wired behind him and a rope around his neck. His bruised and blood-stained skin showed that he had been badly tortured. The back of his shirt had many cuts in it from being whipped. One shoulder of his tattered shirt was still intact. On it was the U.S. Army officers insignia of a full colonel.

The Japanese camp commander was furious and ordered him tied to a power pole. An interpreter shouted that he would remain tied there for three days without food or water. He then would be severely punished. I suddenly recognized that the man was Colonel Breitung, our battalion commander. What he may have done to make them so furious, I had no idea. But being the tough old cavalry officer that he was, I knew that he would not bow down to anyone.

He stayed there in the blistering sun, wired to that pole for three days. He was beaten at each change of the guards. They threw water on him as he passed out to revive him so that he would keep suffering. On the fourth day all prisoners were called out again. We were lined up at attention to watch him be beheaded. After some time standing at attention, a little fat Japanese officer with a big sword came swaggering out. The guards screamed "*Kyotskie!*" then "*Karay!*" which meant that everyone should bow. They then unwired our colonel and dumped a bucketful of water on him and told him to kneel down. Colonel Breitung spit in the Jap officer's face instead. The prisoners snickered in ranks. The guards were horrified, and the Jap officer went into a screaming rage. He ordered the guards to force the colonel to his knees and pull his arms behind his back. Then with one mighty swish of the two-handed sword Colonel Breitung's head came tumbling down toward our feet. Watching his head as it came to a stop and seeing how his eyes kept looking around still haunts me to this day.

Sanitation was nonexistent. There were no latrines. We dug straddle trenches. The amebic and bacillary dysentery spread like wildfire, and the men who caught it could not control their bowels. As a result, the paths leading to these trenches and the areas around them were covered with defecation. Maggots squirmed by the thousands, both on the paths and in the bottom of the trenches. Swarms of fat blowflies blackened the sides of these trenches and swarmed on the weak and filth-covered bodies of the prisoners. Some were so weak that they couldn't even shoo them off. There was no way to bathe.

There was also no privacy. After so many days of confinement, prisoners had talked themselves out, so conversation was at a minimum. Being humiliated, tortured, starved, crowded, and sick, and with each day being a copy of the day before, depression was prevalent.

Often you didn't know the names of most of those around you, nor did you care.

Because of our malnutrition, tropical ulcers developed and festered on our dirty, naked bodies, creating a feasting area for the hungry flies. The fly eggs hatched there and the maggots gorged on the oozing pus. The flies also laid eggs in people's eyes and noses. It became hard to tell if some men were still alive or already dead. There was no relief.

Ode to the Fly (Satan's Little Angels)
Bred in filth, born in filth, nourished on filth,
Evolving into squirming pale larva,
Burrowing into the earth to rest in dark seclusion,
Finally they come forth,
Repulsive, buzzing, minute, with insatiable appetites,

Powerful wings conveying-disease and death to all living creatures, great and small.

As men died, their few and meager possessions became available to the still living. Thus, I was given a mess kit with a lid. When I would draw my ration of rice, I would immediately put on the cover. As I ate, I would lift the lid only enough to get out a bite. Even with this precaution, some of the persistent flies would get in. Dysentery finally got me. In addition, because of the lack of fresh fruit and vegetables, I developed scurvy and pellagra, as did nearly everyone else in camp. Next I developed wet beriberi. My body puffed up with fluids, and my skin took on a yellow cast and blistered under the tropical sun. By that point there were already more than 1,150 graves in this camp.

When the Japs called for a detail to leave camp, I volunteered. My reasoning being that a work detail could be either better or worse but at least it would be a change. They wanted twenty-five men. My eyes were almost swollen shut, and my legs were so swollen that they resembled those of an elephant. The other men looked just as bad, so they took all of us. We were loaded into the back of a truck and hauled south, through the city of Manila, and on down to the little village of Lepa.

When we arrived, we were ordered off the truck and told to line up and to count off in Japanese. A Jap doctor was there to examine us. He spoke some English. He was shocked at our poor condition. He and the Jap in charge had what seemed to be a heated discussion, but they always sounded that way. He then asked us why we were so sick. We told him we lacked food. He said that we would rest for two days and receive *takusan messi messi*—"much food." He told the Jap in charge of us that we would be able to work better if fed better. This turned out to be a good beginning that had a bad ending.

For the first two days we were given the same ration the Japanese soldiers received. On the third day we were lined up and issued picks, shovels, and wheelbarrows. We were marched out to the site where we were to dig down the high ground and fill in the low areas to make a runway for airplanes.

Work went quite well at first. Our spirits were high because of the better food, and we were allowed to set our own pace. Then a Japanese inspection team arrived. The Jap officer in charge wore a spotless white uniform. His aides were bowing to him as though he was some kind of a god. He must have been high up in rank. For a while he strutted around the area. Whenever he would so much as even look at one of us a guard would run over and start beating on that person.

Soon he broke his silence and all hell broke loose. He went into a screaming rage. As he ranted and raved in a shrill, high-pitched voice, the guards started hitting us with whatever was handy. I was knocked down with a blow from a shovel to my head. I was glad I hadn't been hit with one of the pickaxes.

All of the Japs were bowing and bowing to the devil. Someone said they thought he was the homicidal maniac who was called the White Angel. He loved to cut off heads, provided his victims were well bound, shackled, and kneeling before him.

A new group of guards was soon assigned. They were mean. Markers were set out on the runway each day.

We were to level the ground to them. If we made it, the markers were set farther the next day. If we didn't, we were all lined up at attention that evening and beaten and our evening ration was cut in half.

Beatings became almost constant. As we filled a wheelbarrow, a guard would hit us with his four-foot walking stick and make us add more to the load. As we struggled to wheel it along, another guard would follow, hitting us with his stick, yelling, "Speedo! Speedo!" They would not let us stop to rest until the head guard gave the word. The rainy season was setting in and the mud made the work even more difficult. As men fell, they would be beaten until they got up.

My fever soon flared up again. My lungs started to fill with fluid, and I couldn't get enough air. I passed out as I was wheeling a heavy load. Apparently the Japanese doctor saw this happen and had me hauled back to camp in my wheelbarrow. He told the guard that I might have a dangerous and contagious disease that might spread to the guards. He asked to have me and one other guy with the same problems sent to a Japanese clinic in Manila to have us examined. They agreed. When the guards disappeared, this doctor gave each of us a boiled egg. I was so sick I never found out the name of the other person.

  The two of us were loaded into the back of a truck. The doctor told me that we were very fortunate to be leaving, because something very bad was going to happen to the rest of the men. I heard some time later that they were all lined up at attention and machine-gunned.

  Many high-ranking Japanese officers wanted to cut down on the number of prisoners. Japanese Lieutenant

Colonel Tsuje Masanobu encouraged mass murder of POWs. He said his only interest in the prisoners was the number dead. It was apparent that, at that time at least, it was the will of General Homma, the high command in Manila, that all prisoners in Cabanatuan were to die of disease or starvation. Only a few Japanese officers encouraged killings; most of the others just tolerated it. Discipline was left up to the whims of the Jap in charge of a group at the time. His brutality was never questioned.

    Our truck driver did not take us to the Japanese clinic in Manila. Instead we were hauled back to Cabanatuan Camp Number One for the American doctors to take care of us. This was a good thing, because prisoners taken to that Japanese clinic were used as guinea pigs. Maybe this was part of the instructions that the Japanese doctor back at Lepa gave to the driver as we left.

Most of the American prisoners of Cabanatuan Camp Number Three were being moved down to Camp One. Here, the Japs were having about a square mile of native vegetation dug up with pick and shovel to grow vegetables. The camp had been divided into three sections. The men in sections one and two were to work on the farm. Section number three was for those prisoners who were too sick to work. It was called the hospital section. I was taken to it.

Down at the far north end of this hospital section was an old sort of lean-to they had termed the zero ward. It was where the dead awaiting burial were placed. Men were dying faster than the sick guys on the burial details could dig mass graves for them.

August brought the rain in torrents. Our shallow mass graves filled with water. Gases formed in the bodies as they started to decompose. As dirt on top of them turned to liquid mud, the bloated bodies floated up. Sometimes just an arm or a leg appeared. Sometimes the whole body would surface facedown. The grave detail would throw more dirt over them, but as this dirt also turned to liquid, the skeleton-like corpses would slowly float back up again. They literally turned over in their graves. I hate this expression to this day. When I hear it, it brings back those gruesome memories.

Silas Whaley, a man from my outfit, died at 11 p.m. on August 17. I still have the note I wrote about his death in the back of my little New Testament. He had a "disappearing" stomach. He had been featured in "Ripley's Believe It Or Not" back in the thirties. Slender by nature, he was somehow able to draw his stomach and bowels up and out of the way so that you could feel and see the back part of his body cavity. He was real likable and a good friend of mine.

In the weakened condition that I was in, I came down with diphtheria of all things. This was another killer that had started circulating through camp. With all the multitude of ills, men were dying at the rate of one every hour and forty-five minutes, which came to 1,275 deaths in just three months.

Diphtheria is an awful disease. Just a few germs can secrete a large amount of toxin that can paralyze the body. First my throat started to close up, and I had trouble getting my breath. Then my hands and legs refused to function. Then I became completely paralyzed. I was hauled down to that zero ward as dead, yet I was still somewhat conscious.

A number of dead bodies were dumped on top of me. I faded in and out of consciousness. I have no knowledge of how many days I lay there. In one of my semiconscious moments, I remember that some men were lifting the dead off of me to take them to the burial grounds.

When they got down to me, I was thinking of the many men I had seen buried alive and that in a matter of minutes I would be experiencing what they had. Then I heard one of the men say, "I think this guy must still be alive. He hasn't started to rot yet." Another voice said, "Could be. I'll give him some water."

Even though I couldn't move or open my eyes, my mind really perked up. I remember that a horrible thought came to me: "I can hardly breathe, and now they are going to drown me." Someone trickled some water into my open mouth. "Yeah! He is still alive," one of the guys said. "He bubbles. Lets get him out of here."

They hauled me back to one of the hospital barracks and dumped me onto the bamboo slats of one of the bays. I was completely naked. My shoes and clothes, including my G-string, had been removed and given to the living. These G-strings were standard underwear for the Japanese soldier. They were cloth aprons about six inches wide and three feet long with strings. You put them on backwards and tied them in front. Then you pulled the free end up between your legs and flopped it over the strings in front. They put another one on me. It was stained though clean.

A doctor came and examined me. He stuck a needle in my arm and gave me a vaccination. After some time, good attention, a bit of medication that the doctors were able to provide, and the little extra food that the good chaplains brought, I started improving. Then I went completely blind. That was such a helpless feeling. I hope to never go blind again. Stanley, a man from my outfit, came in to see me. He said I needed some vitamins and found some pigweeds, which he steamed for me. I nibbled on them for a few days, and my sight came back.

Another victim of the dreaded diphtheria was my old friend Bob Scorby, a man from my own outfit. Bob was two bays down from me. He was so paralyzed when I noticed him that he was not even able to wipe his butt, and he had a bad case of dysentery on top of that. His defecation had been dripping down through the bamboo slats of his bed, and he was covered with flies.

As I improved I was able to help him more and more. Bob had been a powerfully built man in peacetime. He had been a bouncer in a saloon, but he never drank. "Four ax handles across the shoulders and four ax handles tall" is how they described him. He was always kind and gentle though, a real nice guy. Now he was just a big frame of bones and loose skin.

Bob was a great inspiration to me. He had a strong desire to live. He never swore or held a grudge, and he always had considerable respect for the Lord. He used to tell me that if he ever got out of that prison camp alive, he would never let his stomach be empty again. He did make it back, and lived up to his word until his dying day.

Some news was getting into camp by way of a little handmade radio that was somehow kept hidden from the many inspections of the guards. Also there was a fine old gentleman, Sergeant Bell, a Georgia-born African-American who had connections. He told me he was in his sixties, but he didn't look that old. His second marriage had been to a Filipino woman. They had two little children, both boys. When his wife found out that he was imprisoned in Cabanatuan Camp One she moved herself and the boys into a little deserted *baha* (hut) just north of camp.

Sergeant Bell had made a box toilet for himself and set it up just a stone's throw from the north prison fence. In the evenings he would sit out there. The Japs never questioned this because dysentery was so prevalent in camp.

Mrs. Bell and the boys would walk down the road in the evenings as though going to market. At dusk on their way back the boys would shout names at Bell and throw rocks at him. The Jap guards really enjoyed this. The name-calling was words of love in Tagalog, the boys' native language. On one of the rocks would be a note with the latest news of the war.

As my coordination slowly improved I tried to exercise every one of my muscles to its limit. My legs were jerky and would either move too far or not at all. In one of those uncontrolled jerks my foot hit the wall of my bay and a little bat flew out. The frightened little fellow flew around for a bit and then returned to his original hiding place. I was so hungry that my first thought on seeing him was food, and I grabbed him. The little stinker bit me on the finger. I let out a yell and let him go. Although it was just a little puncture wound, it bled out quite well. One of our doctors came over to look at it. I said, "Doctor, am I now going to die of rabies?" He grinned and said, "No, but after biting you the bat might die."

We were thankful that the rains washed away the defecation on the paths leading to the latrines. The new problem was mud. Since shoes had been taken away from us in the hospital and given to those in the work sections, some of the more ingenious men made go-aheads, pieces of board the size of a man's foot with some kind of a strap over the arch. These were also called clackers. If you backed up you'd slip out of them. They were easy to make but a little tricky to walk in, especially in mud. I had several falls in mine until I got better control of my legs.

The Filipino civilians were trying their best to get food and medicine in to us at the risk of losing their own lives. The medicine was smuggled into the camp in small amounts, but it was a big help to the ones who were lucky enough to get some. The death rate started to slow down.

A new cleanup enthusiasm started in the hospital area, inspired by the doctors. This gave hope and a new incentive for those who were on the verge of despair. They named my barracks the Carabao Café. Four of us got together to chat and eat our small rations. In my group was a marine staff sergeant we called Mac; a tall intellectual we called John Johns; Carl, a Cajun from somewhere in the South; and myself. This socializing was the first I had since capture, and it did a lot for morale.

Carl seemed to have a hatred for blacks. Just the sight of Sergeant Bell made his dark eyes flash with anger. One day he said, "I'm going to cut up that nigger." We were shocked. Bell was our friend and contact for outside news. We asked Carl what he meant. He told us that back home in the Everglades, a gang of whites would run down a black boy and score him up. He told us that they would take a sharp pocket knife and hold the blade so that only about an eighth of an inch would stick out and then score him all over and let him go and watch him run. It was a sickening thought.

We had all kinds of people in camp. There were those who, like Queenie, were feminine. There were thieves and gamblers, bad guys and good guys, and some who had gone completely crazy. I was impressed by the Masons in camp. They seemed to live by a great moral code. I wished I were one. Most of the major religions were represented. Some of these religious men placed the need of others above their own needs, while others were holier-than-thou fanatics.

There were a number of chaplains in camp. The Protestant chaplains worked together and formed a sort of cosmopolitan church. They met after dark, because the Jap guards would come in and break up any gathering they saw. Each chaplain would, in turn, explain his faith. It was very interesting hearing them try to explain how their church differed from the others. I came to the conclusion that the differences were very minor. They all worshipped the same God.

Chaplain Tiffany, the Presbyterian, organized a group for his faith. I joined his church later. I had been baptized a Methodist as a boy, but I thought maybe being baptized twice might help, and I wanted all the help I could get. Our communion consisted of a spoonful of rice we each would save from our last meager chow ration. It represented the bread. A sip of water from a canteen cup represented the wine. It was probably more sincere for us than for some of those who were having communion in a church back home. We each got a membership certificate.

Some New Testaments had been brought into camp and I got one. There was a blank page in the back of it. With a stub of a pencil, I wrote out a complete Thanksgiving dinner menu on that page, including appetizers, side dishes, and desserts. It seemed a proper place for something so wonderful. At that point, food was the most important thing on our minds. Any thoughts of ladies had long since been forgotten.

Around mid-November of 1942, when the rains started to let up, the fly population started to increase again. Many of the weakest men had died. We'd begun dousing the paths to the latrines with water and dust wherever a dysentery patient had the squirts.

We steamed G-strings and whatever other clothing over a barrel of boiling water to kill body lice and their eggs. Also there seemed to be a more fair distribution of our meager rations from the kitchen. I was never able to get in one of the favored cliques, so this was a big help to me.

Our morning chow was a small dip of watery rice called lugao. It was without salt and tasted like paste. The noon and evening meals consisted of a cup of steamed rice and a cup of watery soup of some kind. Anything with protein seemed to get short-stopped before it got down to my level, that is, if there was any. I noticed that my teeth were starting to loosen in my jaw. One of our doctors thought that it could be have been caused by the diphtheria.

The International Red Cross, knowing our plight, had been trying to get food, medicine, and supplies to us, but the Japs wouldn't let them come in. The Japs wanted all provisions turned over to them with no agreement that any would ever be given to the prisoners.

A Catholic priest, a German civilian in Manila, had been frantically trying to get the two to agree: the Japs to give provisions to the prisoners and the Red Cross to trust that the Japs would. The Japs could not seem to understand why a German wanted to help the Americans.

The Japs finally agreed to give us the provisions, but after one shipment was turned over, they decided to lock everything up in warehouses. After more Red Cross persuasion, a small amount was sent to the hospitals. In the meantime we could smell the American food being cooked in the Jap kitchen and the smoke from American cigarettes. It wasn't until in December of 1943, one year later, that I received a Red Cross food box all to myself.

In the so-called hospital, I first met the famous American doctor, Alfred Weinstein. After the war ended, he wrote the great book *The Barbed Wire Surgeon*. Before the war started, Doctor Weinstein had been the top brain surgeon at the Manila Hospital. I wish I could write as well as he. He was not only a brilliant man and a great surgeon but he could also speak Tagalog. He also learned to speak Japanese while in prison camp. And he was a wheeler and dealer, and through his many Filipino friends, he was able to get items and medicines smuggled into camp past the tight security.

Weinstein examined me and said, "We don't have the medication you need, but I do have a big bottle of opium syrup. I don't know the strength of it, but I'll give you a spoonful, and with some food and plenty of rest you should be as good as new in a week or two." He poured the thick brown stuff. It tasted awful.

In a short time, I started to feel sort of hot and tingly. Then I felt giddy. Next, everything looked fuzzy, and I imagined that I was on a flying carpet, floating through the barracks and right out the open window. Then the carpet and I sailed right out into the clouds and disappeared.

When I regained my senses, Dr. Weinstein was shaking me. "You back with us now?" he said. "Guess that's pretty strong stuff." An American chaplain was also there. He introduced himself as Chaplain Frank Tiffany, the Presbyterian minister. He had half a cup of milk and a boiled egg for me. I found him to be a great and caring man. He was a Canadian by birth, a farmer who had answered the call to minister the gospel. There were a number of chaplains in camp, but in my opinion, he was one of the very best. Some turned out to be less than expected. Others lived to help those in the most need.

The Japs couldn't stand to see so many prisoners not working. "Work or die" was their logic. Work parties were being sent out of camp on various details, but the sick were still eating and not working. Officers did not have to work, at least at that time. The Japs had set up some sort of canteen where those who had money could buy a little extra food when available. The Red Cross sent in money for even distribution among the American prisoners, but the Japs set up a pay scale in which officers would be paid two hundred pesos a month for lieutenant colonels, ranging on down to eighty-five pesos for lieutenants. Working privates were to get three pesos per month and noncommissioned officers five pesos. Of course you had to hand it over to the Japs to get the food. More pay meant more food.

    The camp at that time had around three thousand officers in it, one for every five enlisted men. Money is always power, and the officers started using this power. Rank, power, and money went together. The enlisted men in the hospital area couldn't work, so they didn't get any pay. This made recovery even more difficult. I was determined to get better or die trying.

I couldn't help thinking how short a life is, whether it's a day or a hundred years, a whole generation is hardly a flash in eternal time. So many die in war and in other disasters. During our lifetime we each have a chance to leave our mark—good or bad—that in some small way can influence others.

How different the various cultures are. Yet a similarity is there. An American is raised in a free society where every life is precious. In some civilizations, an individual's life is of little importance; however, both the Japanese and the Americans were giving their lives for their country.

Perhaps the difference is in how we do it. In prison camp, a friend's word or helping hand can mean much.

Cruel, harsh words and acts can be damaging, even to the point of making those on the balance between life and death tip the balance in favor of death. I made up my mind that from that point on I would always try to present the good and pleasant things in life. There are always good things. Sometimes they are a little harder to find.

I drew a pan of water and bathed and washed my entire wardrobe, which consisted of only one little G-string. The water stung my tropical ulcers. But then I looked at the many places on my body that were still okay. "I'll make it," I told myself, "no sweat."

The idea of having a vegetable garden became a reality. The Japs were having the prisoners work up land just outside of camp. As the workers started out in the early morning, each was required to grab a pick or shovel.

Men were lined up in rows and made to dig and turn over the sod. Guards followed behind beating anyone who was not keeping up. No one could wear shoes and only a few had a hat. The tropical sun was hot. Farmer Jones was the head prisoner in charge of us, but of course, he was still under the lowest-ranking Jap.

Chapter VII

The Farm

Farmer Jones was a retired soldier who had farmed in the area for years. He knew what would grow there and how to grow it. When war broke out he insisted on rejoining. The original idea of the farm was to have the prisoners grow their own food. The idea was good but things didn't work out that way. The Japs kept most of the vegetables, and the prisoners got the tops for their soup.

The farm area expanded to several hundred acres and many more workers were required. Vegetables of all kinds were grown, including camotes (a Filipino sweet potato), beans, corn, squash, onions, daikons, spinach, carrots, cucumbers, and many others.

The Japs gave orders that a small percentage of workers had to be officers. They were to help the guards supervise the other workers. Also a certain number of hospital patients were to be sent over to join the other workers. To fill this quota the hospital doctors had to send nearly all the patients who had two legs and were able to walk. I was one of them. At that time I weighed eighty-two pounds, exactly half of my peacetime weight, and I still had trouble walking. I was so hungry, even though weak, I was glad to go. It meant that I would get paid five pesos ($2.50) a month. That could buy two eggs. Also I'd have a chance to steal a vegetable now and then, even though I knew I'd get a beating if caught.

We, the selected ones, were marched from the hospital area, under Jap guards, to the work section, and then turned over to the American officers. The guards yelled many instructions to our officers, who bowed in reply. I'm sure they didn't understand what all was said, but it made no difference. Everyone had to play by Jap rule without question.

One of these American officers was my own battery commander, Captain Abston. He looked right at me, but I could tell that he wasn't sure it was me. I was so skinny and had yellow skin and sunken eyes. He looked pretty good. He hadn't lost much weight. I never did get to talk to him.

All buildings in this area were built the same as those in the hospital area: bay floors made of split bamboo. I was assigned to the barracks building, which was the second building from the gate leading to the farm. There were more than a hundred and fifty men in it. My spot was between two guys who acted like zombies. They didn't talk and just did what they were told to do. From the marks and bruises on their heads, they must have been severely beaten more than once. I began thinking that I may have jumped out of the frying pan and into the fire.

There was a tattered blanket for me. I never found out who was there before me and what happened to him. I checked for lice. Sure enough, they were there. I checked the bamboo slats for bed bugs, and sure enough, there were the telltale little black specks, their droppings. I knew I would be sharing some of my blood with them at night. A little childhood ditty came to mind: "If your bed is a little buggy and you had a nightmare, would you take a drive?"

The officer in charge of our barracks informed us that we would be called at early dawn. We would line up outside and be counted. Then we would march as a group to the kitchen to draw our chow. The kitchen had a roof but no walls. No one would be allowed to go inside. We would pass by the two big iron pots, one of rice and one of soup. We would get a dip of each. We weren't to ask for more. We were to quickly get back to the barracks, eat our chow, and shove our mess kit under our blanket. When called to line up, we were to move out quickly. The last man would get a beating. The officer ended by saying that no shoes could be worn on the farm.

    It was now dark. All the farm details had been checked in, and it was time to draw our evening meal. Each barracks lined up as a group and in turn filed by the kitchen and drew our ration: steamed polished rice and a cupful of boiled vegetable tops and water. Also a half cup of weak tea, but I had no extra cup for the tea. The man behind me in line had them add my tea to his cup and gave it to me when we got back to the barracks. I wasn't used to this much food, although it was still a small amount, and I got a bellyache that night. It kicked up my stomach ulcer.

Just before dawn I woke with a start to someone yelling, "*Tenko! Tenko!*" which meant morning roll call. Everyone made a mad dash for the door, but I held back to keep out of the traffic jam. Then a club was jammed into my back from behind and a guard yelled "*Kuda!*" (get going) and "*Domi-doe!*" (very bad). He ran me clear out the door jamming that darn club into my bony spine. Our officers called the roll and reported to the guard that we were all there. He grunted and dismissed us. Our group got in line with those from the other barracks, and we drew our chow.

We gulped down the slimy lugoa, tucked our mess gear under our blanket, and fell out in front of our barracks for another count. It was getting light, but the sun hadn't come up.

We were marched to the farm gate by our officers and turned over to the Jap guards. Our officers went back into camp. These farm Jap guards were an ugly, cruel bunch. Most of them were rejects or injured from combat. It was obvious right from the start that they were out for revenge. They all carried big clubs. There must have been at least ten groups of us with a hundred to a group.

Each group was counted by the Japs in charge of that group, then these guards reported to the *gunso* (sergeant) in charge of all. After the counting they yelled, "*Kiotske!*" (come to attention). Then they yelled, "*Keirei!*" The guards saluted, and we had to bow or get hit on the head again. Then they yelled, "Keirei!" again. We had to bow again. Then they yelled it a third time, and we bowed. The sun was now just starting to show in the east. I whispered to the man next to me, "What's this all about?" He whispered back "Once to the emperor, once to the sun, and once to the man in charge."

Each group was then marched out to their work area for that day. Two or more guards followed behind with clubs. I noticed that there were perimeter guards around the farm. There also were guards with machine guns in the watchtowers.

At the time I thought my first day was a rough one, but I found out later that it was one of the easiest. We were marched out to a field of little radish plants. They were just at the four-leaf stage of growth, but little green aphids were already on the underside of most leaves. We were each given a small can of strong soapy water and a little rag and told to wash all of the insects off. Having been raised on a farm, I knew what this would do to these tender plants. As we each worked our row, we had to keep in line or get whacked on the head.

The guys called one of our guards "Fisheyes" because his glasses were so thick. They had names for all of the guards, because we didn't know or couldn't pronounce their real names. This guard couldn't see the rows and trampled the little radishes much of the time. That day went fairly well. The next day we were sent to a different field. The poor guys who got our radish field were lined up and badly beaten, and they were not permitted to draw their chow that night. It seems that the radish leaves had curled up and turned brown. The Japs didn't care who killed the plants. They just wanted to line up and beat to the ground a whole group as an example to others.

Growing up, I had always thought that Japanese were good gardeners, but these guards didn't know a cucumber from a watermelon let alone how to grow anything. Every time something went wrong they beat up poor old Farmer Jones. The farm kept growing in size, and so did the demand for more workers. The wet season ended and the dry season brought back the heat and flies.

One day my group got the watering detail. My legs had begun working better, but I was sunburned to a crisp. Each of us was given two five-gallon cans with a wire handle and a stick one meter long. We were marched, single file, down to a pond where we filled the cans with muddy water. Then with the stick across our bony backs and five gallons of water balanced on each end of it we had to walk uphill to the fields. The pole soon made open sores on my bare, sunburned back. Ten gallons of water is heavy, and we were barefoot. At the field, we were to walk between the rows and trickle water onto the plants from the cans. We were sure to get clubbed by a guard if one was close because it seemed we could never do it the way he wanted it done.

A day of rest finally came. Most of the guards went to Manila to exchange venereal diseases with the native women. We could rest our aching muscles and wash our bleeding feet. That day I found out which shooting group I was in.

The entire camp had been divided into ten-man shooting groups. That is, if someone in your group escapes the other nine would be shot. The idea was for us to police our own. They counted us several times at the gate, and at one count a member of our group was missing. We had been on the water detail. There was much excitement both with the guards and with us, and they began yelling and shoving. We nine were marched into a small, empty windowless cellblock where others had been kept before being executed. The door to the cell was then locked. We were informed we would be shot at sunrise, a very important time of day for the Japanese.

The whole camp was made to watch the executions. During that long night we didn't sleep or talk. If there was any sobbing, I didn't hear it. We were each absorbed in our own thoughts and praying. I wondered if my folks would ever find out how I died. I guess it didn't really matter. I thought how much they had done for me over the years and how ungrateful I must have seemed. A million thoughts went through my mind. We all had suffered so much, and what had it gained us? Maybe those who had died early were just a step ahead of us.

My thoughts went back to the old bum who had befriended me on the dock in San Francisco. "I'll be with you in spirit," he'd said. I wondered if I was about to see him.

As dawn broke, a faint streak of light started to show through a crack in the east wall. We heard the men lining up for breakfast. There was the usual counting and the sound of many feet. Next the work details were being formed, and then everyone was marched out of the gate. We heard the kiotski and the three keireis and then the guards yelling and beating on some prisoners. Then came the thumping of bare feet fading off into the distance.

The eastern sky was brightening. Our eyes had grown accustomed to the dark, so the little light that was filtering through the crack seemed to light up the room. We were crowded together, watching the upper edge of the sun appear over the horizon. I could hear my heart beating loudly; it sounded like nine hearts pounding. No one said a word.

We watched as the big ball of fire rose and completely cleared the horizon. Then someone whispered, "Why are they making us wait?" Another whisper: "They're great at torture, even at the last hour." The sun rose higher and higher. There was no ventilation, and it started to get very hot inside.

It must have been midmorning when we heard approaching footsteps. A key turned in the lock, and a Jap opened the door. An American officer was with him. Our officer said, "You guys can come out now. They found the guy hiding in the swamp, and they're still torturing him." We were marched out to the farm without food or water, but we weren't complaining.

The man who had escaped was forced to dig his own grave as part of his torture. He was beaten on all parts of his body and, finally, bayoneted in the bowels. Guards ordered some of our men to cover him with dirt as he writhed in agony. He smothered to death in his grave.

The Japs fired a shot over his grave. An interpreter explained that the shot fired was to honor him for being a brave warrior because he had fought so viciously when caught. He had jerked the gun away from the guard who found him and had bashed the guard in the face with the rifle butt.

More acres were cleared and added to the farm. By now the Japs had more vegetables than they could use, so they decided to haul them into Manila and trade them for rice. They'd also begun adding some to our soup but not nearly enough. It was obvious that they wanted to keep us overworked and underfed. We'd be easier to control that way. The hospital ration had been so small that it was just a slow road to death by starvation even for one who might otherwise be well. It didn't mattered to the Japs if we were working or dead.

With the worker's ration and stealing a vegetable now and then, I had started to gain a little weight. Then came the day that I ate too much. My group was on a weed-pulling detail in the cucumber patch. It was easy to eat some carrots unnoticed when in the carrot patch. You waited until the guards looked the other way, pulled up a carrot with a weed, bit off the bottom of the carrot, and shoved the rest back into the ground. It would usually keep on growing.

But the cucumbers were big. The smallest was over a foot long and three to four inches in diameter. I was so hungry I thought I could eat a whole one. When I saw my chance, I snapped one off and took a big bite out of it. The spot where I had taken out the bite showed like a light among the green leaves. Sliding the cucumber along under the vines I bit off big pieces as fast as I could swallow the last. I managed to get a good three-fourths of it down. By then I was nearing the end of my long row. It was almost noon and time for all to head into camp. The guards were moving up behind, looking for signs of anything partly eaten. I had to eat the rest or get caught and severely beaten. Worse yet, I'd likely get my arm broken for stealing. Somehow I was able to get the rest of it down except for what was still in my mouth. They lined us up on the dike at the end of the row. Some of the men got clubbed. I wanted to throw up but knew that I had to hold it.

The guard we called Air Raid came over to see what was going on. Air Raid was one of the meanest of the mean guards and a little higher in rank. He carried a large club and was generous with it. He talked to the guards who had done the beating then proceeded to beat these men all over again. One of the men was knocked out cold from a blow to the head and had to be carried halfway to camp before he regained consciousness. He was then able to stagger on in with some help.

Finally I was able to get the rest of that cucumber chewed up and swallowed. Man, was I miserable! In camp

I was able to upchuck some of it but not enough. By midafternoon I was sick. Even the smell of the plants made me prickle all over. By evening I had the staggers and my hands and feet were getting numb. I had to have help getting through the chow line. I traded my evening ration for two cigarettes. I didn't smoke, but they could be traded back for chow at any time.

    The next morning I was completely paralyzed. Luckily no guard came through the barracks that morning. The American officer in charge of our group asked the Jap guard to let me stay in. The Jap came in and checked on me, slapped me around a few times, and then said I could stay. One of our doctors, after questioning me, diagnosed my condition as cucumber poisoning. I quite agreed with him. This only lasted one day. I tried to play it longer, but I just wasn't a good enough actor.

The area of the farm now included some of the old rice-growing plots. These had small dikes around them so the rice could be flood irrigated. There were also gigantic termite hills. Some were twelve feet high or more. They had been there for many years. The Filipinos considered them good luck and would never tear them down. They were on high ground so they didn't get flooded, and they had become homes for not only the termites but also for rats, mice, ants, and snakes. The Japs wanted them torn down and the dirt spread out.

We used picks and hoes for this. These mounds were hard. As we hacked them apart, ants boiled out and bit our bare feet and legs. There was some real fancy dancing at times. Mice and rats scurried in all directions, and snakes came tumbling out. Most of these snakes were cobras, which the Japs considered a real delicacy. The first Jap to see a snake was entitled to it, but the prisoners had to run it down and catch it alive for him.

As this racing and yelling was going on, the guards got almost hysterical. You would think they were watching a baseball game. I suppose it did look pretty funny, guys wearing only a G-string, running after a slithering, twisting snake, trying to pin it down with a hoe.

As one of our guys was trying to overtake a viper, the expectant owner ran along behind, hitting and screaming at him. When the snake finally stopped, it coiled and spread its hood for the fatal strike. Our man pinned it down with his hoe and grabbed it just behind the head. The Jap, in his excitement, reached for it. Just as his hand got close our man released his grip, and the snake grabbed the guard's hand just back of the little finger and started to pump in its deadly venom. It would not let go. The other guards were cheering and we were cheering, but our cheers were for the snake. After much frantic shaking and pulling, the guard finally bit the snake in the back of the neck, paralyzing it. He then took off his bayonet and sliced through the heal of his hand where the fangs had entered and started sucking out the poison. Blood covered his face as he sucked away.

    We watched, expecting him to drop over dead. One of our men offered to hold his rifle for him but he shook his head. He took the sweatband from around his head and wrapped it tightly around his hand. He then motioned for us to get back to work and took his snake and sat down on a dirt dike. No other guards went to check on him. He lived, but the snake died. The next day he was back with his hand wrapped up and meaner than ever.

The honey detail was one stinking job. Everyone hated it. We had to carry two five-gallon cans filled with the waste from the latrine balanced on a stick across our bare shoulders. We did the oriental shuffle so it wouldn't splash all over us as we carried the raw sewage to the farm. As we walked between the rows of vegetables, we gave each little plant a dip of the stinking stuff. We used a four-ounce can tied to the end of a stick as the dipper. With a dipper in each hand we could fertilize two rows at a time. This stuff was too strong at first, and a lot of the plants died, which caused a lot of men to get beaten. Farmer Jones was able to talk them into cutting the solution with water, which worked much better.

[[COMP: Story break.]]

Oh, how these Japs loved to beat prisoners. It gave them a chance to express their power. Being cruel was a way of life in the Japanese military. The privates first class would beat the privates, the corporals would beat the first class, the sergeants would beat the corporals, and the officers would beat the sergeants. This was a privilege and the way to gain respect: bow to anyone above you and kick hell out of anyone below you.

They brought some new Japanese recruits into camp one day for the more experienced soldiers to train. My guess is that these boys ranged in age from twelve to fifteen. They were scared stiff. It was one of our very few rest days, and I was able to watch the start of their training. They were just outside of the prison fence. A Japanese first class was training them in face movements. He showed them how to do the manual of arms, the right face, and the left face, but when it came to the about face, one of the boys just couldn't do it. After several attempts the first class started screaming. This made things worse, and the poor scared kid started getting his feet all tangled up. A corporal wearing a white, short-sleeve shirt and a big sword strapped to his side slowly walked up and took over. The first class bowed to him and got out of the way.

The corporal got the boy out in front of the others and showed him how to do it. Then he quietly gave the boy the about face command. The boy was scared stiff. Sweat was pouring from his face, and he was so tense he was almost rigid. As he tried to do the command, his feet tangled up and he fell flat. The corporal yelled for him to stand at attention. As he did the corporal yelled the about face command again. The poor kid was so scared by this time that he locked up and didn't move at all. The corporal yelled, "*Bacaro!*" (stupid) and went into a screaming rage. He grabbed the gun away from the boy, knocked him down, and beat him on the head with the rifle butt until he was dead. The corporal then told the first class to take over as he, the corporal, swaggered off. We stood there in shock with our mouths open, trying to believe our eyes.

The first class saw us standing there inside the fence and ordered us to come out. He made us dig a grave for the boy. We were really rushed. He made the other recruit carry the boy over and lay him, facedown, in the grave. We had to stand by with our shovels. All recruits were ordered to march by and spit and kick some dirt on him. We were ordered to cover him with dirt, and then we were marched back into camp. This was such a haunting experience that the memory of it has stayed in my mind as clear now as the day that it happened. I had heard that in the Japanese army, any Jap could take the life of anyone under him, and now I believed it.

My group was assigned to the woodcutting detail one day, which was much better than the farm. Our guards rode behind us in trucks as we were marched to a wooded area. Half of us were given axes, and the other half would load the wood onto the trucks. We could change back and forth from cutting to hauling as we wished. This worked out quite well.

I found some plants that had little green peppers on them. I bit into one of the peppers and almost immediately got a big white blister on my lip. These little fellows were only about the size of an apple seed, but they were sure hot. I carefully picked some and wrapped them in a big leaf and took them back to camp. By smashing just half of one into my watery soup and pouring the soup over the tasteless rice, I could give the ration some flavor. What an improvement!

One evening, after receiving a painful beating on a farm detail (I never found out what the beating was for), I pulled my mess kit out from my tattered blanket and didn't hear the sound of my little spoon. After lifting the lid and feeling around in the dark, I found that it was gone. I really valued that spoon. It was about half the size of a teaspoon, but using it made my rice seem to last longer. Also, I had sharpened one edge of the handle so that I could shave with it. A work detail had shipped out that day, and my guess is that my little spoon went with it.

I broke off two twigs from the scrub tree at the end of the barracks to use as chopsticks. In line for chow that night, as I passed the big iron pot that cooked our rice, I singed the twigs in the fire to burn off the bark and bugs. They worked great. I used them to rake in the rice and greens, and then I slurped up the liquid.

Early one morning my ration of watery broth had something strange in it. It was something kind of slippery and fuzzy, kind of like the stuff my mother called "mother of vinegar," a harmless mold that would grow on the top of old vinegar. This thing though held together in my mouth. I spit it out and left it in my mess kit to be checked at noon when there would be light.

Back in at noon I opened the lid. Yuck! What a stink! It was a partly decomposed mouse. The guts and lower skin had rotted away, and in their place was some kind of a jelly-like stuff. The heavier parts of the skin remained though most of the hair was missing from these patches. "Why didn't you just swallow it in the first place?" a fellow next to me said. "Your stomach would never know the difference."

Some darn American came up with the bright idea of making a water wheel to lift water from the stream up into an elevated trough from where it could flow by way of gravity to the different fields. This was to replace the backbreaking job of carrying those heavy water buckets on poles across our backs. The idea would have been great, except in the hands of the Jap guards, everything turns out bad.

    The Japs liked the idea and ordered it made, but they didn't want to supply any of the needed material. Our men were to make it out of native bamboo and rattan and five-gallon square watering cans. It was to resemble a

Ferris wheel and was to be powered by prisoners walking up the spokes. The water buckets would be placed where the seats usually are. As the wheel turned it would dip each bucket into the stream, fill it with water, carry it up and over the top, and dump it into a bamboo trough.

At first the thing was too light and flimsy and tipped over. I was in one of the groups that was to walk the rungs, but the water was heavier than we were. A guard jerked me off and beat me with his stick because I was too light. They extended the rungs on either side of the buckets so that two men could fit on each rung. They were able to get the water part way up, but then the weight of the water would carry them up and over the top. They would have to jump off or end up in the water. Then the Japs would beat them. I was moved to other details, so I don't know if they ever got it to working.

November 1943 brought new hope. Rumors were flying that we had won some big sea battles and that MacArthur's lead forces were moving up from the south. The word was that we'd be home by Christmas.

The Japs had begun giving us some vegetables in our soup and the rations were more uniform, seldom cut as punishment for some minor incident on a work detail. I had gained some weight. I would guess that I was up to nearly a hundred pounds. The rains had let up and the sun, as yet, was not too hot. November and December seemed to be the cooler months of the dry season that was starting again.

Some men came back into camp one day and said that their guard told them that *toxan* (many) Red Cross boxes were on the way and would arrive before Christmas. We really wanted to believe this, but with so many past disappointments it was hard to do so. But hopes ran high; morale perked up. Even the most depressed seemed cheerier.

In mid-November Red Cross boxes *did* arrive. Hallelujah! Prisoners got so hysterical that you'd think we were crazy. And maybe we were a little. In fact, I'm sure we acted that way. I had always tried to be the levelheaded one, but not this time. We lined up by barracks groups and marched by the big stack of boxes. Each man was given a box.

They weighed a good twelve pounds and contained a can of corned beef or spam, butter, coffee, powdered milk, chocolate, raisins or prunes, sugar, jam, soap, cigarettes, and toilet articles. We were rich. It was our first real food since the start of the war. Rations had been skimpy or nil on Bataan, short on Corregidor, and then much, much worse in the prison camps.

The cigarettes were buying power, and it only took one or two at a time. It was hard for me to understand why some had such a craving for tobacco. I planned in detail the amount I could eat each day. I rationed each thing to make it last as long as possible. I would sprinkle only a sifting of the powdered milk or chocolate over my rice. What a difference it made! The old saying that rice is a wonderful food because anything you do to it improves it sure is true.

I even traded a cigarette for an old pair of shorts to cover my G-string. I also got a pair of shoes. Boy! I'd become a big New York strutter. I felt so good I could almost like a guard (a dead one). The prisoners had begun talking again, sharing big dreams of what we would do when we got back home. At this point none of us had doubts that we'd be getting back. That soon changed.

The farm details didn't seem so bad any longer. Some of the guards didn't like the change in the prisoners and took offense at it. If you so much as even grinned at one, you got the hell beat out of you. Even the short, bow-legged little guard we called Charlie Chaplain (he wobbled when he walked) got real mean. The one we called Donald Duck had gotten mean some time before, when he found out that the famous American movie star, Donald Duck, was just a cartoon character.

Christmas Day came and went. Everyone was singing Christmas carols, even me, although I couldn't carry a tune in an airtight bucket with the lid sealed on. It didn't matter though. The good feeling I had is what really counted. It had always bothered me somewhat that when praying I seemed to be always asking for something instead of being thankful for what I still had—mainly, life, faith, and hope. Now I had a lot to be thankful for.

January and February of 1944 came and went. I worked on the farm, first on one detail and then another. The mood of the guards set the mood of the day. The news of the war now, for them, was not good, and we prisoners were the easiest victims to take their revenge out on. The center of the group was usually the safest place to be except for times when the whole group was lined up at attention and clubbed. They got their exercise at our expense.

March through June was unbearably hot and dry. With all the watering and the fertilizer, the vegetables grew big and fast, but the sun was hard on bare skin.

From several odds and ends of cloth I made a stupid looking hat. The Japs laughed at it and joked between themselves. I didn't care. My head was covered. They even called me over one day and took my hat and passed it around and had a big laugh at it. They did give it back.

Rumors of all kinds surfaced in June. One was that we would all be shot. One was that they were going to trade us for Japanese prisoners. One had us being shipped to Japan, where the Japs would use us as human shields until we were killed off. It seemed that if you didn't like the rumor you heard you made up your own.

Chapter VIII

The Hell Ship

War seemed to be getting closer. The guards were screaming and acting excited and watching the sky a lot. Rumors were flying through camp that there was a big sea battle going on. Details were being formed and sent out of camp. Most were to go to Japan. The time of the "Hell Ships" had begun.

On July 1, 1944, I found myself in one of the groups to go to the "Land of No Return," as we called Japan. They checked our stool samples to see if our dysentery was active. Mine checked out okay, so I was placed in a group with ninety-nine other men. They made several groups of a hundred men each. We were hauled like livestock to Bilibid Prison in Manila.

They gave me a new G-string and a baggy pajama-type top and bottom. These were much too large. The material was coarse woven stuff that scratched and must have been made from rice straw. It was a pale yellow-green color. The buttons on the top part were made of hard-pressed paper. The pants had drawstrings but no buttons. I wondered what would happen to this stuff if it got wet.

We spent the night and the next day at Bilibid Prison. Groups were arriving and moving out, destination: Japan. Chow was the usual rice and watery soup, no better or worse. We were given the glass rod check for dysentery again. But at that point the Japs' attitude seemed to be that if we could walk we would go.

On July 3, my group was one of several groups that were marched under a blistering sun down that familiar road to the Manila docks. Memories were with us of the atrocities that had occurred along this same road after our capture. Also, many had died since then, and many more were still to die.

    We each had an issue of cooked rice and a canteen of water and our mess gear. Some had a bag of belongings. I must have had shoes of some kind, since I don't remember the hot pavement burning my feet. I do remember the heat on my bare head.

    At the docks were many ships of all shapes and sizes. Some were so dilapidated it was surprising that they were still afloat. As we were herded up to one miserable looking cargo ship it reminded me of the stock yards back in Omaha, Nebraska, of the way cattle were driven into enclosures and jammed together before they were to be slaughtered. The difference being, we would be feed for the sharks instead of for people.

As we walked up the plank to get on, I noticed that the deck was jammed with contraband from the Philippines, such as old car bodies, rolls of wire, and junk of all kinds. All was tied down to keep it from sliding around.

There were two holds. Each had raised planking around it about a foot and a half high. A rope netting was draped over one side for us to climb down into the dark stinking hole. It was a good eighteen feet or more to the bottom. The group ahead of us was the last to be jammed into the back hold. They were packed in like sardines, standing room only. I could feel the heat radiating up from them. They were already screaming for more air. There was no breeze, and it was deathly hot.

I was glad the guards finally decided that they couldn't pack any more in and our group was moved on to another hold. As we started down the ropes some of the guards shoved men over the side, causing them to fall the full depth and land in agony. The floor was filthy with manure and steaming, wet, moldy bedding from horses. I don't know how they ever got their horses in and out of those holds.

When I reached the bottom I saw a rack suspended at the back, about six feet above the floor. Two men were getting up on it, and it looked like there could be room for one more. I shoved my way through sweaty bodies and reached it just as the man ahead of me was trying to get up on it. He was too weak and couldn't make it. I asked the guys who were on it if I could join them. One said, "Is your canteen full." I told him that it was. He said, "Come on up," and he gave me a hand.

More and more men were forced down into the hold until it too was packed solid with sweating, bony bodies. They were jammed so close together that they were almost directly breathing what the men next to them exhaled. Anyone who went down had little chance of getting back up. I gave thanks for my perch. At our level there was more oxygen and less carbon dioxide in the air.

By the time the loading was completed the sun had lowered enough that the temperature seemed to stabilize. I'm sure it was well over 100 degrees Fahrenheit. No food or water was sent down that night. It was that old "train car treatment" all over again, only this time it would last much longer.

As the sun sank below the horizon and daylight gave way to darkness, the sounds of agony lowered to a dull murmur with an occasional outburst or shrill scream of pain. We on the rack had to draw up our legs because desperate hands were trying to drag us off. One of the other two men had a small rope. With it we tied ourselves together and to the frame of the rack, in hopes that we would still be there in the morning. We still didn't know each others' names. In such closeness names were not needed.

During the night a breeze came up and pulled some of the bad air out, replenishing the oxygen. I dozed off, and just before dawn I awoke to the sound of a blood-curdling scream, followed by a tremendous amount of commotion. Someone yelled, "Kill the son-of-a bitch!" At daybreak it was reported that several had died during the night.

Rumors of cannibalism spread, with claims that thirsty and starving men had attacked fellow prisoners too weak to defend themselves. There were so many different explanations it was impossible to know what really happened. Some asked the guards if we could send the dead up to be dumped overboard. They refused.

The tropical sun rose high in a clear blue sky the morning of July 4, 1944, and the heat in the hold rose with it. There were three outdoor-type privies that hung just over the edge of the deck above. Men were asking to go up and use them but were emphatically refused. An interpreter said that they could not be used in the harbor but that we would be sailing soon. Then two five-gallon cans were sent down on ropes. When full, one man was permitted up to dump them. He had to dump them right beside the privies. I was surprised to see how few men had to use them. We were so dehydrated and had eaten so little food that our bodies had little to give. I went more than two weeks without a bowel movement. When our man came back down, he said there were many ships in the harbor, both coming and going. There seemed to be much confusion, and a guard had slugged him when he looked around.

Sometime during the midmorning, several five-gallon cans of rice were let down. I'm sure that our potty cans were two of them. There was not near enough rice to go around. We three on the rack decided to just stay put. The location was more valuable than trying to get a handful of rice that we probably wouldn't get anyway. After about an hour the same cans came back down with what looked like weak tea in them. One of the guys with us on the perch had an empty canteen. We agreed to hold his place while he filled it, and then we would share it. It took some doing for the two of us to fight off those who were determined to take his place. He worked his way back to the tea, but it was gone before he got to it. We helped him back up onto the rack. He was completely exhausted.

By noon, with the sun directly overhead, the heat seemed unbearable. Someone said that somebody had a thermometer that was reading 120 degrees. I don't know if that was true, but it was sure hot. The breeze had stopped and the air had become suffocating again. We could hear the men in the hold behind us chanting for water and air. Then our group picked up the chant. The guards yelled for us to shut up. One of the guards fired his rifle down into the group. I don't know if he killed someone or not, but he got a real chewing out from one of his noncoms for shooting into the old wooden hull of the boat. The deck hands were ordered to cover the holds with the heavy rain tarps to try to quieten us down. This completely shut off all circulation, and the hold became even hotter.

Moisture evaporated from my body like moisture leaving a grape as it turns into a raisin. I filled the lid of my canteen with water. It was hardly a swallow. The canteen was hot, as was the water. Conversation had stopped, and the men below us had begun collapsing on top of each other. They lay as they dropped, in tangled heaps, like dead men on the field of battle. My vision blurred. I passed out.

When I came to, it was dark. I could hear the sound of the boat's engine and feel the vibration of the propellers. The tarp had been rolled back. Fresh air was circulating, and it was cooler. There were bright stars in the sky above. As the boat gave a tilt to the left I could see the Southern Cross.

A few of the tangled bodies were starting to move. It was creepy. I wondered if these ghost-like forms were really spirits of the dead trying to get their bodies to have just one more go at life. It didn't matter. Those alive today might be dead tomorrow anyway.

I wondered what happened to the life of a plant when the plant died, or, say, a bird? Does each have a life after death? Do they have their own God? Where does energy hide? The atmosphere is full of sounds—music, speeches, insects communicating with each other. Radio and television receivers can receive and send our transmissions, but what happens to thunder once it has rumbled away? Do these resonances lie dormant? I started to feel very small and insignificant. I wondered if life was worth the price I had to pay, yet I was afraid of death.

I pinched myself to jar my senses back, but I could not feel the pinch. One of the men next to me stirred a bit and seemed to be awake. I said to him, "Are you still alive?"

"I must be," he replied. "If I were dead I wouldn't be so miserable."

Our old boat made a sudden jerk, as if it had hit a submerged rock outcrop or had been hit by a torpedo that didn't explode. There was a lot of excitement up on deck, but I couldn't understand anything the Japs were saying. Then the stars above gradually rotated about 180 degrees.

By morning we had dropped anchor. Pee cans were let down again. Most of the prisoners were up now. They seemed to be less crowded. Those who no longer could get up and were being walked on. Many had removed all of their clothing except for a pair of shorts or a G-string, because of the terrible heat.

Again the guards picked one man to follow up the pee cans and to dump them over the side. When he came back down, he reported that we were back in Manila Bay. One of the guards had given him a smoke and let him look around a bit. He said the bay was still full of ships. He had no information as to why we had returned.

Whenever that darn canvas cover was pulled over the hold, as it so often was, and the oxygen changed to carbon dioxide, some men went completely crazy. A few became temporarily cannibalistic. One of the men on my rack let out a yell one day. A crazed guy had grabbed his leg as it hung over the edge of the rack and was trying to bite off his toes. We pounded the guy in the face until he finally let go. The toes were badly chewed and bleeding. It wasn't long before they became infected. What a hell of a situation to be in with no medication.

When deprived of absolutely everything, the first thing one craves is oxygen. The next is water. Then comes faith in something more powerful than man himself. Next comes food. The last is companionship. One person alone can't protect himself from the power of another who has gone completely berserk, but with others, there is more strength. It is hard to paint a mental picture of what those conditions were like unless one has gone through it himself, and God forbid that such should ever happen to anyone again.

I don't know how many days and nights passed before we finally got on our way. There were several attempts to sail, only to be brought back into the harbor. There were a lot of American submarines just off the coast. The prisoner-of-war ships were not marked as such, so there was no way for the subs to know that there were prisoners aboard. Records show that many of these ships were sunk, but ours made it. Ours probably looked so old and small that the subs, no doubt, didn't want to bother with it.

A strong storm moved in from the China Sea. Our old boat, while still at anchor in Manila Bay, pitched and rolled. The rain came down in torrents. Everyone was trying to catch drinking water in anything he had. Then the Japs pulled that darn tarp over us again, pulled up anchor, and headed out to sea. Once out on the open waters the old tub was tossed around like popcorn in a corn-popping machine.

Everyone got sick, but of course we had nothing in us to throw up. I didn't think we would make it, but somehow we did. Our boat was just one of the group that was trying to weather the storm to avoid attack by the submarines. Some of the junk on deck broke loose and slid around. No doubt some of it went overboard, and maybe some of the deck hands went overboard too. At least I hoped so. It was a long and wild ride.

Eventually we ran out of the storm area and entered a port in Formosa. The dead bodies that had been stacked against the forward wall of the hold had been scattered during the storm and had to be restacked. There was no way of identifying them. All dog tags had been taken away from us when captured. Names had been replaced with numbers for the records, and with the naked dead there was no way of finding out the number. Some were so discolored and decomposed that they were far beyond recognition anyway.

Historical records show that captured Africans who died aboard the slave ships were cast overboard. We too were slaves, but with our captors, we were also the enemy. I don't know why the skipper refused to cast them overboard. The smell was terrible. It may be that he had to deliver as many bodies as he had loaded, dead or alive.

In this bay other ships were lined up for a turn at the dock, so they could load salt into the area below the holds to add more ballast. We sat at anchor for several days. At last our boat got its turn at the dock. It chugged into position and tied up. It was hot, but not nearly as hot as it had been farther south. The stink in the hold was much worse by now and the lice were bad. I occupied myself by popping them between my fingernails.

Some of our men were mentally gone. They were to be avoided. You could see the danger in that faraway look in their eyes. I felt sorry for them. Their suffering had been too great.

The Japs started giving us more food, or maybe it just seemed like more because there were fewer of us eating it. They sent down the five-gallon tins of water until everyone had all he wanted and all canteens were full. I noticed that the Japs had started wearing masks over their noses because of the awful smell rising up from the hold. It was starting to get chilly at night, and some of our men pulled up pieces of clothing from the filth on the floor. All of it was saturated with defecation, urine, and that wet, rotten horse manure bedding.

We were allowed to take turns to go up and use the privies that were suspended over the starboard side. It was great to breathe that clean air full of oxygen. It was early morning, and the sun was just breaking over the low mountains to the east. Two parallel planks were laid at an angle from the dock to the deck of our ship. A long, single line of workers was approaching.

These workers were either captives or coolies carrying the salt. They were oriental people of some kind. They were very thin and taller then the average Japanese. There were men and women, all in black kimono-type jackets and baggy pants tied at the ankles. All were barefoot. The men wore flat-top hats with wide floppy brims and the women had black scarves tied over their hair. Each had that familiar stick across their shoulders with a wicker basket suspended on each end. The baskets were rounded full with coarse salt. These people were expressionless, and they moved like robots. They shuffled up the slanted plank, dumped their baskets of salt into the metal chutes that sent it down to the area below the bottom of the holds, and trotted down the other plank. Moving like a column of ants, these poor people formed a continuous line, bearing those heavy loads of salt day and night without letup until the job was complete. This took the greater part of three days and two nights.

    Our ship then pulled out and dropped anchor in the bay again. We had an occasional rain that helped to wash a little of the filth from our bodies, but it added to the slush underfoot. I wondered how much was dripping into that salt below.

The distance from the Philippines to Japan must be around one thousand miles, more or less. The island of Formosa lies about halfway between. It took the ship nearly two months to make that distance. It was in and out of harbors many times, often the same harbor. It would drop anchor in little inlets for days at a time, apparently trying to avoid the U.S. submarines that were active in the open waters. All this time we were starving for air, water, and food.

I, for one, had some hellish dreams during these seemingly endless days and nights. When the oxygen levels are low and carbon dioxide levels high, one's mind acts in strange ways. Why I still remember some of these dreams so vividly is a mystery to me. I have tried to shut out all memories of prison life, but it is impossible. I did, however, keep it pretty well bottled up for many years, but now with encouragement from family and friends, I am recording it for them and for future generations, for whatever use it may be.

One dream was of a huge green fly with slanting yellow eyes and big shark-like teeth. It was bulging with ready-to-lay eggs. It sat above me, watching and waiting for me to die. The suspense would wake me up or bring me back to reality.

In one I was looking at myself in a big mirror. I saw myself eating my left leg. When it was eaten, I ate my right leg. Then I ate my left arm. All that was left of me was a big swollen belly and one arm that was trying to stay away from my big wolf-like teeth. Then my stomach exploded and my arm and legs popped back out and I was whole again.

In another dream, I was set down at a table that was loaded with the best food of all kinds, but my mouth was wired shut and I couldn't eat.

Another was that of sinking down and down in deep hot water and a Jap pushing me even deeper with a long pole. Other Japanese were watching and grinning silently as I gasped for air.

One was of a mosquito drawing out every bit of my blood. It would swell up larger and larger until it would burst open and all of my blood would flow out onto a rice field and fertilize the rice crop.

Then there was the awful one in which the Jap guards would beat me with clubs and chop me with swords until I was nothing but a big pile of hamburger. Then they would serve this hamburger to their troops with rice. With every bite they took, I would scream with pain.

A final one was of an explosion that destroyed everything and everyone on earth except me, and there was nothing for me to eat.

These were repeating dreams. There were many more, all of which caused mental suffering that added to the physical suffering.

The final part of the voyage to Japan is a complete blank in my memory. I apparently spent those last days in a state of shock or a coma. I don't even remember getting off of the ship. My first recollection of actually being there was of lying on a concrete floor in a barn-like building. It was remarkably clean for a barn. Through the center of the floor was a trough that somewhat resembled the kind in our cow barn back home on the farm. It was used to catch the cow manure. One of the prisoners told me that we were in Japan on Kyushu, the southernmost island. It was cold. He helped me to get up. I staggered as I tried to walk, and I coughed a lot. It seemed that my lungs could only take in small breaths of air, but that fresh air certainly was welcome.

As I looked around I began to realize that we all looked like skeletons, sort of like an animated Halloween scene. Every Japanese looked like a fat, roly-poly Buddha compared to us. The wind was very cold, and my little G-string—my entire wardrobe—provided no warmth at all.

Those wearing the dirty rags wet with urine and manure that they had pulled from the filthy floor of the ship must have been as cold or colder than I was. We all spent the night in that open-door barn, huddled together for warmth. I don't remember being fed that night, but we probably were.

In the morning we were marched out, lined up, and counted. We were then divided into groups and marched out for breakfast. This was a new and strange experience. We had to walk along a path, in single file, between strands of wire—one on each side of the path—that were about thirty inches above the ground. These wires were charged with electricity. A Japanese interpreter told us not touch the wire. "It is *domi domi*" (very bad), he said. We were being controlled by an electric fence, just like cattle.

One of our men staggered into the wire. He immediately locked up, completely immobile. The man behind him grabbed him to pull him free, but he too froze. Some quick thinker jerked the towel from around his neck and flipped it over the first man's arm and pulled him free. This, in turn, freed the second man. Both men went into shock. Of course the Japs thought this was real funny.

The food, served at the end of the path, was good. It was the first time that I had soybean curd. We each received a two-inch cube of it, a full scoop of steamed rice, and a dip of vegetable soup. The soybean curd was kind of tasteless but high in protein. No one traded it off. The two men who were in shock and lying prone on the path revived after getting some warm soup down them.

The guards then counted us off again. I was in a group of two hundred. We were told that we would be working in a coal mine, where we would be warm. They failed to tell us how warm it would be. We were marched a short distance to a railroad track where there were flat cars waiting for us. There was nothing to hold on to.

It was a beautiful day in the early part of September 1944. The little train on its narrow tracks puffed along through the countryside. My belly was full of food. My mind had finally cleared up, so I could think again. I filled my lungs with the fresh, cool air. I gave thanks to God. It was a great feeling.

Our train ride ended at the city of Omuda. We were ordered to get off and line up. They counted us and seemed satisfied that we were all there. We were then turned over to a new bunch of guards. These guards made sure that we understood that they were tough and mean. They rattled off a lot of new rules that were to be strictly followed, and they conveyed that punishment would be harsh. We were then marched off to the coal mine area, where they planned for us to spend the rest of our lives doing slave labor.

Chapter IX

Fukuoka Camp 17

The distance from train station to camp was short. It felt good to exercise in the crisp air after the long ride on the flat cars. We clicked off the distance in cadence, marching again as soldiers. The guards were impressed. We were halted at the gate to the prison compound and ordered to display everything we had on the ground in front of us. This wasn't hard to do since we had practically nothing.

After a quick check, the *gunso* (sergeant) in charge of us ordered, "*Mi-Yat-Sumay!*" (forward march). The big gate swung open. We marched in, right up to a little Japanese *shoko* (officer). He was standing on a box, but his head was only on level with ours. He had a gigantic sword strapped to his side that made him look even smaller.

Our gunso gave us the halt and face right command in Japanese. We knew these commands well. Then he yelled "*Kyotski!*" (attention) and "*Karay!*" (salute). I was on the right of the front rank, and without thinking, I came to a hand salute. Immediately a club came down on top of my head from behind. It nearly put me on my knees. Several other men who saluted received a like blow. I heard an interpreter yelling from somewhere, "Prisoners do not salute, they bow."

As the stars cleared from my head, I saw that little turd Asao Fukuhara on the box, holding a full hand salute as he slowly returned it from one end of our group to the other. Then he brought it down so quickly it looked like he would snap off the end of his fingers. The gunso yelled, "*Naray!*" (end of salute).

Then the shoko started a long spiel in a high, shrill voice punctuated with obvious outbursts of rage. An interpreter stood on the ground beside him but was unable to keep up. This made the shoko, who we soon learned was the camp commander, even more furious. I, for one, was glad that I couldn't understand a word he was saying. One thing I remember was the interpreter saying, "You work or you die!"

I could see out of the corner of my eye that the compound was enclosed with a high board fence. The boards were vertical with no place to get a foothold. There were a number of long, narrow, low buildings. I noticed other prisoners. Some were white and some black with white, kinky hair. All were standing at a distance, obviously interested in seeing who was in the new group. Some of these men were Englishmen, some were Dutch, and we found out later, some were half-Dutch and half-Javanese.

A shriek of, "Karay!" from our gunso brought my attention back to the shoko, who was giving us another sweeping salute, ending in the same abrupt manner as his first. He then stepped down from his box and strutted off with his big sword clanking against his boot with every step. We now were a part over seventeen hundred prisoners of war of Fukuoka Camp Number 17.

The Japanese interpreter could not speak English much better than I could speak Japanese, which was pretty darn poor. He was telling us that we would be receiving *takusan* (a lot of) *messi messi* (chow) and new uniforms. Next we were marched off in single file and ordered to drop all of our filthy rags in a pile to be burned. Then we were dusted from head to toe with a strong insect powder. I don't know what was in that powder, but it sure did burn like fire, especially in our open sores. In a few days, those open sores scabbed over.

Each of us was given one new G-string, pajama-type pants, and a top of a coarse woven material made of something that looked like pale-green straw. It was so coarsely woven that when looking through it and moving it from side to side you could see things as though looking through a picket fence while driving by. It was scratchy. Also, each was given two thin blankets made of woven paper. We were not to get them wet. And we each received a straw 6-by-9-inch pillow that was about 4 inches thick. It was very firm; you couldn't smash it with your fist.

We were assigned to sleeping barracks, about fifty men to each. The interior of these buildings was somewhat like those in the Philippines in that there was a six-foot walkway down one side of a sleeping deck. Both ran the full length of the building. The sleeping deck was covered with closely packed 2½-by-6-foot woven straw mats that were 2½ inches thick. We were thankful that the building was cool.

There were outdoor water faucets by every other building. We filled our canteens and washed our mess gear from these. We were to remain quiet at all times. Guards walked the interior of the camp. We could not leave our building except to line up for chow or a lecture, to get water, or to march off to work.

This first night in camp we lined up for the evening meal, and as we passed by the cook shed we each were given a little wooden bento box for our rice, a small bowl for our soup, and a pair of chopsticks. The box was about half the size of a cigar box.

As I drew my box of rice, the man dipping it said, "Hi, Graham! How are you doing?" It was Staff Sergeant "Pappy" Yokum, the mess sergeant from my old Battery G of the 60th Coast Artillery (AA). It was sure good to see him again. He had a few bruises on his head from being slapped around by the guards, but otherwise he looked fairly good. At least he was not as bony as the rest of us.

"Hi, Pappy. You look like hell. How long have you been here?" He grinned back and said, "I *am in* hell, and you look like the Devil himself. I hardly recognized you. I'll pack the rice in your box good and tight. It will make quite a difference." I had to move on because a guard yelled at me for talking.

I learned later that Pappy had come into camp with the first detail of American prisoners back in August of 1943. There were five hundred of them, and they opened this camp to start the slave labor in the condemned coal mine. It had been condemned during peacetime by Japan as being too dangerous to work because of cave-ins. With the demand for coal for the war efforts it had been re-opened by the army and was now being worked with prisoners of war and with Korean civilians as overseers.

After drawing our chow, we had to return to our barracks to eat it. I had picked the eleventh sleeping pad from the door. I didn't want to be in the first ten. That could become the group to be shot if someone should escape, yet I wanted to be close enough to be able to hear the guards as they called out orders. No more being last one out and getting the daylights beat out of me.

The man who bunked next to me was a Dutchman. I never found out how he happened to end up in our group. He was well educated and could speak French, German, and English very well. He had been a high school teacher back in Holland before he was required to do his time in the army. He was a noncommissioned officer.

He told me a lot of things that I had never heard before. One was how Holland colonized islands. He said that the Dutch soldiers sent to these islands were required to take several native women as their wives. The native men were isolated from the native women. These native women would then bear children who would be half-Dutch and half-native. He said that the Black Dutch, the ones with black skin and white kinky hair here in camp with us, were some of these offspring. He said that their mothers had taught them to hate the Dutch. They could all speak Dutch as well as their native tongue, and some could even speak English. They had been well schooled.

Our first morning in camp started at early dawn with *tenko* (morning roll call). We lined up outside our building for a count. A guard had been assigned to each building, and he made the count. The guard then made his report to the gunso in charge. We were then dismissed to draw and eat our ration of rice and watery soup and to use the *benjo* (latrine). Just as the sun started to come up, everyone had to go through the bowing routine: once to the sun, once to the emperor, and once to the camp commander. Next we had to do calisthenics. As we completed these, the little camp commander clumped out in his rubber boots that were obviously way too big for him. His big sword banged his leg with every step. I hoped it would trip him, but it didn't.

    The gunso in charge screamed "*Kyotski!*" (attention) in such a frantic voice that it sounded as if someone was killing him. As the little *shoto* (officer) in his little short-sleeve white shirt and his baggy pants climbed up on his box, the gunso yelled, "Karay!" This time I remembered to bow to the little turd. He gave another screaming lecture that we would work the coal mine twelve hours a day for as long as the emperor needed us. Again, if we didn't work, we didn't eat. We would have a rest every tenth day if we had worked hard. He blabbered off a lot of rules and regulations, all repeated by the interpreter. Each rule was followed by a severe penalty if disobeyed.

Out of the corner of my eye I could see three POWs on their knees by the gate. Their hands were tied behind their backs, and they had bloody heads and shoulders. Punishments would always be severe. As Mr. Turd got down off his box and clomped away, one of our men was pulled out of ranks and beaten. None of us knew why.

Our first day in the mine started with the usual formality except that it was earlier, and the little camp commander didn't show up. It was a cold September morning. Wearing only scant clothing and barefooted, we marched down the cinder-covered road to the mine, a distance of about a kilometer. The cinders were sharp and cut our feet, but the little wooden lunch box tucked under our arm was comforting.

A fairly large building covered the entrance to the mine. Inside was a shallow cement bathing tank filled with hot water. The tank was about a meter deep and ten meters in diameter. The late-night shift was in it as we passed. No words were dared exchanged between us.

We stacked our scant clothing, and then wearing only our G-string, we drew our mine lamp, cap, and an acid battery. The lamp attached to the hat just above the bill. The battery was strapped behind us on a little belt buckled around our waist. An electric cord connected the lamp and battery. On that first day I drew a leaky battery that dripped acid on my bare skin. By the end of the day, I had an acid burn that took days to heal. After that I made sure that I got a good battery.

A wooden canopy covered the pathway from this building to the mine entrance. On the way we had to pass through a low-swinging wooden gate to get to the rail cars that would carry us down into the mine. We also passed a little birdhouse sitting on top of a post. It supposedly contained the Mine God. It was an absolute requirement that everyone who passed it show great respect by reverently bowing to it. If we offended the god, something terrible might happen in the mine. I didn't need any more bumps on my head, so I bowed, but in my mind I was bowing to my Christian God.

As we approached the dark open mouth of the mine, I could feel the warmer, sulfur-laden fumes its depth belched up at us. I knew the direction would reverse as the outside air pressure and cooler temperature changed. The crew cars were on train tracks. These little cars were somewhat like those used on roller coasters back in the States. They were chain driven by a big drum that was powered by a high-voltage electric motor.

We climbed in and filled the hard bench seats that were worn smooth from years of usage. There were no seat belts or bars. The Japanese guards remained topside. The Oriental on the control lever was either a Korean or Japanese civilian. As we were seated he called out, "*Abani!*" (danger) and shoved the lever into gear.

There was a clank and a jerk and away we went at breakneck speed, down, down, down into that dark hole. I felt like my heart was in my mouth. I wondered if we would ever be able to stop. The air became heavier and hotter as we descended into the guts of hell. The pressure on my eardrums became so great that all sound seemed to cease. It was hard to take in a breath. The little car was vibrating so hard it seemed it would disintegrate. I was so scared I couldn't even pray. I hoped that I hadn't offended

Mine God in the little birdcage. We began to level out, and occasional electric lights partly illuminated the turns.

We passed by laterals where some of the men of another shift were working. We could see their headlamps dimly lighting the veins from which they picked the black layers of the loose and dusty bituminous coal. This type of coal is soft as compared to the harder anthracite coal. It also produces much more smoke and ash.

There was a grinding of wheels in the heavy layer of coal dust that littered the tracks, and then a squeal as the little crew cars came to an abrupt stop, causing us to slide off our bench seats. By now my eyes were burning. There was a pounding in my ears that kept pace with the beat of my heart, but I was starting to pick up some sound from outside my body.

"*Aut-su-ma-rie!*" a voice shouted. We all got out and lined up. A group of Korean overseers appeared out of the darkness. They, too, were wearing only a G-string and the headlamp. Their oily brown bodies shone with perspiration. Each counted off the number of us that he wanted on his work crew and motioned for us to follow him. As near as I can remember there were nine of us in this first group. Three were given scoop shovels, three were given pickaxes, and the others were not given any tools. I had received one of the shovels, and I was sorry that I hadn't waited. But I found out later that I had the better job.

We followed our leader down several laterals, making so many twists and turns that I knew I could never find my way back out. I just hoped he could. We came to a lateral that had settled so much that there was only about a three-foot space between the floor and the ceiling. We crawled through on hands and knees for nearly fifty feet. There were groans and pops in the formations above us as the area above continued to settle. Water seeped through cracks. Bits of pulverized rock oozed out from the layers of slate rock. Our Korean leader said it was "*domi domi*" (very bad). Pointing up he indicated that we were under Nagasaki Bay. This part of the mine had been condemned as being too dangerous. With their war, Japan needed much more coal, so the "condemned" sections were being reopened with slave laborers, both POWs and Koreans.

Pillars of tree trunks, a good foot or more in diameter, had been brought in for support. They had been placed vertically and several feet apart along the length of this lateral in hopes of holding up the ceiling. The tremendous weight of the formations above had squashed these timbers, which had splintered out at the center into shapes that resembled paper Japanese Lanterns that the Japs sometimes hang around their tea gardens.

I thought about those pressed leaf fossils that archeologists dig up, and I wondered if we might end up like that. We weren't in the depths of hell—we were under it!

Just before we emerged into a more normal lateral there was a deep boom from the section ahead of us. The tunnel walls vibrated. "*Mito!*" (blasting), announced our leader. "*Hi-ya-ku! Hi-ya- ku!*" (Hurry! Hurry!) our leader called back as he took off at a trot. Our creepy tunnel had been a shortcut to a work area that had been prepared for us.

As we approached, a dense cloud of black coal dust filled the air. The light from our headlamps could not penetrate it. Coal dust entered my nose and lungs. Gasping for breath, I jerked off my G-string and tied it around my face. This helped. Gradually the coal dust settled to the point where things became visible. I noticed that all of us were coal-black, and our eyes and teeth showed up very white. We could only identify each other by voice. We had become real coal miners.

There was an empty coal car on the rails, which led up the long, long incline and out of the mine. An avalanche of coal had been blasted from the wall just ahead of us. Above it, shelves of slate rock jutted out like fins from a gigantic fish. It was the job of our pickax men to climb up on this loose coal and break off these rocks. It was dangerous work. The sharp rocks would come tumbling down at their feet. It required quick foot action to avoid them.

The men without tools had to stack these slabs of rock into pillars until they reached the ceiling. It was backbreaking work. My job and the job of others with shovels was to scoop up the loose coal and fill the coal car. There was, of course, no breeze, and the coal dust hung in the air with every swing of the scoop. I coughed and sneezed and had to constantly wipe the coal dust from the lens of my headlamp.

Hour after hour we worked. Finally a buzzer sounded, announcing time for the midshift lunch break, but our lunch boxes were nowhere to be seen. Every inch of the entire area was covered with a heavy layer of coal dust. Our Korean leader punched around with his wooden staff until we heard it strike the boxes. With considerable pawing around and much coughing in the clouds of dust, we finally found all of them, as well as our canteens. After that we always stored them in an adjoining lateral. It was a lesson well learned.

Going to the benjo was another experience. The Korean leader indicated by slapping his butt and pointing that we were to go into a nearby empty coal lateral to relieve ourselves. I dashed in first, not because I needed to but mainly just to extend my lunch break. Heavy sweating and scant rice rations do not make using a toilet very necessary.

As I crept back over the jumble of broken rocks that were blanketed with coal dust, a putrid odor told me that the place had been used many times before. Yet there was no sign of any human waste around. It was steamy hot.

Wiping the dust off of my headlamp, I could see the area ahead quite clearly. There, looking straight at me, was the largest cockroach I had ever seen. He was fat and a good seven inches long, and he was feasting on another cockroach. As my light hit him, he seemed to rise up on his hind legs, holding his victim in his front feet, with his cannibalistic eyes reflecting in my light. His long feelers were groping in my direction. As I swung my light around, I could see dozens more in all sizes. On the ceiling there were large white crickets. These also had long feeler antennas, but they had no eyes. I got out of there in a hurry. Anyone dying in that place wouldn't last long with that hungry horde.

As each coal car was filled, we had to push it by hand up the track to where it could be hooked onto the conveyer chain that would pull it up the steep grade and out of the mine.

By the end of that first day I was so tired I just wanted to lie down in the dust and sleep. Then I thought of all of those hungry cockroaches, and with a burst of energy, I moved to the head of our group as we stumbled out to the waiting crew cars.

The ride back up was slow and long. Our ears popped, and our eyes burned. Everyone's feet were sore and bleeding. Those who had been hoisting rocks had some bad-looking fingers. Everyone was black. The chopsticks in our little rice boxes started to rattle, a good indication that our hearing was returning. We were so tired that no one spoke.

"*Hi-Ya-Ku! Hi-Ya-Ku!*" yelled a Jap guard as our crew car came to a halt. It was dark at topside, nearly twelve hours since we had started this shift. It was cold and windy. We were herded into the big family bathhouse.

The interpreter inside told us that there were strict rules for bathing and they must be followed. Rule 1 was that no one was to get into the bath tank until he had washed himself clean. Rule 2 was that we were to wash outside of the tank by dipping a wooden bucket into the tank and while still on the outside of the tank pour the water over ourselves and rub ourselves clean. Two men were to check each other and be sure the other was clean. Rule 3 was to place the bucket back on the rack and get into the water very slowly. It was very hot. Rule 4 was no *benjo* in the water. Rule 5 was at the sound of the whistle everybody was to get out and dress.

He was right. The water was *very* hot. He was wrong in saying we would wash until clean. There was no way we could get all of that coal dust off. It was in our pores. We were able to get the loose stuff off so that we at least wouldn't blacken the water. The heat sure helped those aching muscles. It's no wonder the Japanese like their baths so much. It would have been real easy to fall asleep in there.

A whistle blew, and then someone yelled for everybody to get out. I was so weak that I had trouble crawling up over the side of the tank. We put on our cloth G-strings, straw pants, and pajama-type tops. They were damp from the steamy air of the bathhouse. We lined up in our original groups and counted off. The cold night air was even more chilling as it blew through our damp clothes. Our bare feet soon became numb from the cold ground. We stumbled along in the dark over the cinder-covered road that led back to camp. Sharp pieces of cinder penetrated the open cuts of our bleeding feet. Our skin had been softened by the hot bath.

At the gate the guards exchanged their usual screaming, then we moved in like a herd of tired oxen and were counted again before being released for chow. The three men who were being tortured as we left on our shift were still there, kneeling on rocks, their hands wired behind their backs. They were wet and shivering from having water dumped over their bare bodies. Slow torture is a Japanese pleasure.

Pappy Yokum wasn't at the rice pot at that hour, so I got the same ration as the others, which, of course, was only fair. We then headed back to the barracks and our straw mats and paper blankets. I was so cold and tired that I didn't feel any bed bugs feasting on me. Maybe they didn't like cold bodies and the taste of coal dust.

It was still dark when we were called out again the next morning. That day followed the same pattern as did the many days that followed. After the tenth day, a day of rest, we were changed to the second shift. No one had a watch, but it seemed to me that the first shift ran from six in the morning until six that evening. The second shift ran from two in the afternoon until two the following morning, and the third shift ran from ten at night until ten the following morning. These hours included the time of going to and coming from the mine and the bathhouse time.

At the beginning of each shift we continued to bow deeply to the Mine God. Anyone not showing the proper respect was immediately pulled out of line, beaten with sticks, slapped and kicked, and then made to go back through and do it over. I was hoping that some little bird would build a nest in it. If one did it would probably be a jailbird.

As days dragged on, it was hard to tell one from the other except when something unusual happened. On each shift, as our crew car came to a stop at the end of the rail-track, Korean overseers would meet us and select their work crew. Those of us who could still do a fair amount of work were in demand. The foremen apparently were rated on how much work their crew did.

Some of our men were suffering from mental problems, beatings, depression, malnutrition, etc., and they couldn't keep the steady pace required. As a result, they were constantly beaten and yelled at. It didn't take long for the foremen to decide which men they wanted on their crew.

A plump, jolly, shiny, little Korean foreman always greeted us with a big "Ohio!" meaning good morning or hello. For some unknown reason he always picked me as one of his crew. At lunch break he would sometimes share boiled soybeans with us. As we ate, he would tell us stories and jokes in Korean. He would laugh and laugh at these. We couldn't understand a word he said, but we smiled and nodded as if we did. When it looked as though we would not make our quota, he'd grab a shovel from one of us and shovel coal like a madman until all the cars were full. We would pat him on the back and tell him how strong he was. He would beam from ear-to-ear and flex his arm muscles for us. He was in good condition compared to us.

One time when he was shoveling, a Japanese mine inspector quietly walked up and saw what was going on.

Someone called attention, but it was too late. As the Korean saw those three red horizontal bars in the inspector's headlamp, his mouth dropped open, and his expression changed to one of pure horror. He stood there petrified, too frightened to even bow.

The Jap inspector said in a quite voice, "Domi domi," and asked the foreman for his name. When we came up out of the mine at the end of our shift, we saw our foreman surrounded by Japanese supervisors. We never saw him again. After that we had some nasty foreman.

Everyone in camp knew about the Mito Man—the dynamite man. He was a screaming maniac. He had killed at least one of his crew that we were aware of, and he had beaten others so badly that they had to be carried out of the mine. I don't know if he was a Korean or a low-cast Japanese, but he was really off his rocker. Even the Korean foremen were afraid of him. He would sometimes chase one of them with a stick of dynamite in one hand and the dynamite explosive cap in the other. Then he would burst into his hideous laugh.

At times he would call for a crew of only one man, and at other times he might take three or four, depending on how many jackhammers he would be using. The men with the jackhammers had to drill holes into the slate rocks, and then tamp in one or more sticks of dynamite. The fuse would stick out at least eighteen inches. Mito Man determined this length. Several clay wads were then tamped in to hold the explosion inside so it would blast out the rock.

There were times when a stick of dynamite would be wet with sweat. That was a sign that it was very sensitive and could explode at any moment. I had learned this back home on my dad's farm when we were blasting stumps for our winter firewood.

One shift, when helping him, I saw one of these sweating dynamite sticks and showed it to him and told him it was very domi domi. The crazy fool laughed and licked the oozing nitroglycerin with his bare tongue, slapped it into my hand, and, giving me a hard shove, motioned for me to tamp it into the prepared hole. I pushed it in with the utmost caution. We didn't have to fuse it, knowing that it would explode as the other charges went off.

My fear and hatred for him grew with each shift. He must have read my thoughts, because he started beating me more, and I knew my days were numbered. When we blasted down layers from the ceilings, he always sent one of his helpers in to tap around. He listened to the sound and could tell which rocks were solid and which were dangerously ready to come crashing down.

One day he sent me in, and as I turned my light up and onto a big section above my head I could see that it was ready to drop. He was watching from the entrance to the lateral. I turned my headlight into his eyes so it would blind him and tapped the solid rock just beyond the section, which sounded good and solid. He came in. Just as he was well under it, I gave it a mighty jab and jumped back. The section that came down must have weighed several tons. It was so large I could hardly get up over it and out through the nearly blocked opening. I thought I would be in real trouble when we came off of the shift that night, but nothing was ever said. It was considered just another mine accident.

Chapter X

Winter

November of 1944 was cold. Snow blanketed the land and turned into slush as our bare feet trudged the road to and from the mine. The Japs were carefully monitoring our diet to make sure that we would continue to be undernourished. Their intent was to let the weakest die, thus saving food and feeding only those who could work. Coal was badly needed to power their war efforts, which were not going too well for them. We heard that there had been a great sea battle in the south, but that's all we heard. We could assume that they must have had a great loss or they would have been bragging about another victory over the weak Americans.

The sick were usually taken to an area they called a hospital, for experimental surgery. Few ever returned. We all knew this and continued to slave away, hoping that war would end before we would.

One of the men in my group got his leg crushed by a slab of rock as he was picking it down. He had to keep working until the end of the shift, and when he got up topside they wouldn't let him take a bath because he was so bloody. We took turns helping him back to camp. One leg was badly broken, and both were badly lacerated.

Our kitchen crew patched him up in camp. They tied sticks of firewood on each side of the break and wrapped it. At the start of our next shift, he was pulled out of ranks and assigned to an aboveground cleanup job. I was impressed. This meant that he would be breathing clean air.

My lungs had been filling up with fluid, and they seemed to be getting worse fast. I came up with the idea that if I could get a topside job I would have a better chance. At least I wouldn't die from pneumonia, which had already killed thirty-five our men.

I waited until near the end of the next shift to smash a foot. It had to be real. At the time it seemed to be a foolproof idea. While no one was watching, I picked up the largest slab of slate rock I could lift, balanced on my right foot, placed my left foot on a rock, and brought the slab down full force on it. My aim was good, but my reflexes were better, and I brought my foot back just before the slab hit. A sharp edge cut the top of my foot but that wouldn't get me any sympathy.

Determined, I picked up another slab and went through the same process. This time I concentrated on keeping my foot in place. It worked, and man, did it hurt! But I was sure that I had smashed every bone in that foot.

The noise attracted the attention of one of the other guys. "I saw what you did," he said. "If that gets you out of here, I'm going to do the same thing." He was impressed, but I was in real pain. The Korean foreman came over to see why we had stopped working. He looked at the bloody mess and said, "Domi domi," and told the other guy to get back to work.

At the end of that shift the guys helped me to the crew car. When we arrived at topside, the Korean foreman reported my accident to the guards. Some Jap, who seemed to be in charge, came over and looked at it. Then he said, "Right foot, accident. Left foot, no accident. You work." For many days after, I regretted that stupid mistake. The foot got infected but eventually healed. I had to work every shift as though I had not been hurt.

Then my group got assigned to a log-carrying detail. We had to drag logs through low laterals and wade through rivers to get to the other crews who were building timber supports for holding up crumbling ceilings in some newly opened coal veins. We had to tie a short rope around the end of each log and, on hands and knees, drag them through a low, condemned lateral, then float them through the flooded places. My left foot was hurting so badly I had to put all my power on the right one.

A few days later my lungs were so full of fluid that I passed out standing in line to go out to work. I was carried over to the little dispensary they called a hospital, where I was dumped onto a real bed that didn't have a mattress. An American POW was on the other bed, dying from spinal meningitis. I said, "Hi, Mac. What's your name?" He said, "Who gives a shit?" That's all he ever said. He was sweating terribly and was all drawn up with his head nearly touching his knees. He was just skin and bones.

Some time later, a Jap would-be-doctor and his assistant came in. They looked at the poor soul and jabbered to each other for a bit before deciding to make him lie flat on his back. One held his hips and the other grabbed him by the shoulders. They both pulled hard. The poor guy let out a blood-curdling scream. I heard his back snap as they bent him straight. And then he died.

I started a bad coughing spell, and as I bent over the side of the bed, fluid poured from my lungs. They looked at me and then left. They must have thought that I didn't have long to live. After getting rid of that stuff I could breathe better, so I crawled off the bed, went back to my barracks, and rejoined the work group. They never checked up on me.

My hopes now were that I could live to see my thousandth day as their captive. As near as I could figure it, that would be January 29, 1945. At the mine I consistently wore a cloth over my nose to strain out some of the coal dust. At one time I had wished that I could work in the steel mill, which was aboveground work.

I mentioned this to my Dutch bunkmate who worked there. "Forget it, mate," he said. "You wouldn't be alive today if you worked there. Those guys have to shovel coal into open-door furnace ovens. Those who get too weak to shovel or who pass out are thrown into the fire and vaporized in that awful heat. Remember, that heat turns iron into molten steel."

He was right. I just had to keep alive one day at a time. Rumors were circulating that battles were going in favor of the Allies. Perhaps the Japanese were finally getting the licking they deserved for starting this war. Many thousands had already died, and many more would die. Would I be one of the latter? Only time would tell. I started praying more and thanking the good Lord that I had made it this far.

In March 1945, Allied planes started bombing somewhere to the north, and the Japs were getting mad as hornets. No longer were they acting as though Japan was invincible. Some were meaner and others seemed to be more thoughtful, perhaps seeing the handwriting on the wall, so to speak. It must have been in May or early June when dive bombers started dropping incendiary bombs on towns in our area. One night they bombed the area right up to our camp, but no bombs fell inside. As they finished their runs, the last plane made a low flight right over us and dropped out a small cylinder that contained an Aerial photo of the area. Our camp was marked "POW CAMP."

May 6 was my completion of three years as a POW (1,096 days). It was sometime during this month that some of the guys broke into a camp warehouse where the Japs had stored Red Cross boxes. These boxes had been sent for us, but we never got any. The Japs were feeding their own men with them.

This occurred when my shift had been down in the mine. On returning to camp, we saw the four accused being tortured. By then they were so covered with blood that they were not recognizable. They were kneeling on sharp rocks with a pole squeezed behind the back of their knees, hands tied behind their backs, and holding rocks in their mouths. If they spit out the rocks they would be beaten severely, and the rocks would be forced unmercifully back in. At the end of our next shift, two or three undergoing the punishment were still alive. As we stood there in formation being counted, I saw a guard peeing in the face of one of these poor souls.

Around the third week in May there was a lot of visible air activity. The Japs made us dig a large bomb shelter, a death trap. It was a long trench, wide and fairly deep, but it had thin poles placed across the top of it, and these poles were stacked with dirt. One close bomb could cause the whole thing to collapse, burying everyone.

Maybe that was the intent. There had been rumors for some time that the Japs would not let any prisoners back into American hands. In fact, one guard had said, "Men die."

It was great to see the U.S. planes bombing. Prisoners had been dying from starvation, suffocation, disease, beatings, beheading, torture, firing squads, smashed skulls, bayoneting, experimental operations, torpedoes, drowning, butchered while still alive, and, also, in the Hell Ships, those rumored to have been killed by other prisoners just to drink their blood. It was no wonder that prisoners cheered these bombings with, "Give 'em hell, America!" and no longer feared for their own lives.

Smoke from the incendiary bombs and the burning buildings blanketed the morning sky and drifted with the shifting winds. Again, dive bombers hit areas right up next to our camp. One bomb landed so close that an electric power pole just outside the camp toppled, breaking the electric wires. As these wires made contact with the ground, sparks flew and the wires recoiled back up into the air. We had been lining up to draw our chow for the next work shift, but the insulation caught fire, so we all backed away.

To our shock, a little Jap guard came running out with a pail of water and threw it on one of the bouncing, burning electric wires. Electricity leaped from wire to bucket and grounded through the Jap, and he went tumbling like a beach ball. I don't know if he lived or died, but we all cheered.

Word was out by now that all Japanese were going to fight to the last man if the Americans invaded. In fact, information captured at the end of the war bore this out. It was recorded in a confiscated Japanese journal that regardless of the circumstances, all POWs were to be destroyed. Any manner of annihilation was to be used. This could be done in an individual basis or in groups. No trace of the destruction should be visible.

It was obvious that the United States had overcome the setback we had at the start of the war. The first two years had been Japan's. They had spread their empire from the Aleutian Islands just off the tip of Alaska, down the International Dateline to the Gilbert Islands, then westward, taking in the Solomon Islands and Guadalcanal, the north half of New Guinea, all of the Netherland East Indies, on north to occupy Burma, Hong Kong, and Manchuria.

The holdout of Bataan and Corregidor had been a real pain for them because it barred the use of the big Manila Bay, which was to be the hub of this whole expansion.

Their boasting had almost stopped. In 1944 and 1945 their attitude had changed from strutting confidence to vicious hatred. They experienced an evil delight from prolonged torture, including butchering prisoners alive to watch their inner organs work as they died. Most of these victims were selected at random.

Hope, faith, and determination were all we had going for us. We prayed, as did our loved ones back home.

Hitler had died on May 1, 1945, but we knew nothing about it. The war in Europe had formally ended May 8, VE Day. We didn't know that either. Around this time one of the men being punished for taking the Red

Cross food finally died after being beaten for a full week. He had received no food or water all that time.

Things were getting worse in the coal mine too. There was bombing above ground and earthquakes below. One of my last days in the mine was so bad it haunts me to this day. It's hard to tell even after all these years.

The shift I was on was working deep in one of the most distant laterals. We were shoveling coal when a big quake started. A real nice blond American was with me. He was just one swell guy, younger than I, always full of hope, and looking for some good in everything.

Following a big quake came several small ones. Sections of the ceiling started dropping. Our Korean foreman had taken off. I said, "We better hightail it out of here too," and he agreed.

Then came a monstrous quake. The ground heaved and rumbled, throwing both of us down. I had a seasick feeling in the pit of my stomach. There was the deep sound of grinding rock. Debris came tumbling down around us. A rock knocked off his headlamp and broke the bulb. All mine lights went off, and the big water pumps stopped. Water started rising, pouring in through new cracks in the formations. My dim headlight was the only light. "Lead the way," he said. "I'll keep my hand on your shoulder. We'll make it."

There was so much powdered rock and coal dust in the air that my little light didn't reach very far. I cleaned the lens with my G-string, and we started. He had a good firm grip on my shoulder. Just as we were coming out of that little lateral, without warning, the whole right wall moved in on us. Fine rock caught my legs but the solid rock wall closed in on him from the pelvis down. He didn't scream. He just gasped, "It's got me. I can't move." As I turned my light down I could see he was pressed like a fossil from the waist down.

"I'll go for help," I said. "Can you hold on? I'll need the light."

"You can't help me," he said. "No one can. Just get yourself out of here as quick as you can. I'll pray for you." I stood there for a moment, not knowing what to do.

"Go, damn it!" he yelled. "There's more coming down. Save yourself. You can't save me."

I don't remember coming out of the mine. The last thing I remember is that moment with him. I know his body is still there, and I know his soul is with the Lord.

Chapter XI

The Atomic Bomb

The morning after the first atomic bomb had been dropped, the one on Hiroshima, everyone in camp was called out for morning tenko by screaming, hysterical Jap guards. We were rushed quickly into formation with disregard as to what group we belonged in. They didn't even count us. Stragglers were being run into line with guards hot on their heels, beating them every step of the way.

The little arrogant camp commander was already on his box, impatient and furious. His interpreter was at his side. The commander started his spiel before we even had time for the official bowing. The translation was so fast that it was hard to understand. The message that came through was: "The enemy, the Americans, have dropped one bomb from one plane. The bomb weighed 2½ kilos. It floated down on a little silk parachute the size of a handkerchief. It has killed many thousands of women, children, and hospital people. Starting now, you will receive no more food. You will work as long as the emperor wishes." It's not clear how he came up with the description of the bomb.

With that, he stepped down from his box, nearly falling, but no one dared to laugh. He strutted off. We waited, standing at attention. No one seemed to know what to do, especially the guards.

Finally we were all sent back to our barracks. We were instructed to not talk or go outside, not even for water. A guard was said to have told someone that Russia might declare war on Japan. That was hard to believe since we knew that Japan and Russia had an agreement with each other. A day later, on the eighth, we found that it wasn't a rumor after all; Russia *had* declared war on Japan.

Midafternoon of the seventh we were given a half-ration and shifts were sent down into the mine. In the mine, there was a big rush to get the loose coal loaded into the coal cars and up aboveground. It was "Speedo! Speedo! Speedo!" all of that shift, and it was a very long shift. We worked the main laterals close to the rail tracks, the section of rails that made the steep ascent out of the mine. At the end of that shift, we were hungry, dehydrated, and completely exhausted.

When we returned to camp the morning of August 9. We were *so* weak and hungry, but we received no food. There was obvious turmoil in camp. Guards would give an order then change it and give a different one. Higher-rank Japs screamed at the lower ranks. Again we were not counted, just dismissed to go to our barracks.

I dropped down onto my straw pad with the horrible thoughts of that night of the earthquake in the mine. I wondered how high the water was now in that lateral. I wondered if ~~he~~ my friend was still alive—if he had drowned or if more rocks had taken his life. Had his suffering stopped?

I felt sick, but I had nothing in me to throw up. I prayed. I wondered if his parents would ever know how he died. I knew that I could never tell them, and that I would never try. My throat was dry, but sweat poured from every pore of my body. I had the shakes and a splitting headache.

Midmorning of that same day, the air raid sirens started wailing. This was not unusual. There had been a lot of air activity. Guards came running through the barracks, yelling for everyone to run to the death-trap air raid shelters. "All in," they shouted. "No one in sight."

I had to join the group, but I remained near the entrance, determined to be where I could get out in case a bomb collapsed the whole darn thing. I would rather take my chances with the bombs than buried alive.

We heard the sound of one or more big bombers. They were very high above the clouds. Then the "all clear" sounded. As I looked up, I saw one long, silver plane high overhead, only a glimpse of it through an opening in the clouds. Then it disappeared from sight. I wished they would bomb the camp instead of just flying around.

Others were coming out of the so-called shelter when there was a *brilliant* flash of white light. It was so bright that it was painful to the eyes. As in the case of sheet lightning, we couldn't tell where it came from. I heard no sound of an explosion or thunder. There was an earth tremor, and then a strong hot wind blew in from the west, the direction of the big city of Nagasaki. Everyone stopped talking.

Next there was a much stronger wind that came from the opposite direction, the east. It was so strong that it toppled over some of the men. It upset barrels of trash, blew boards from the compound fence, moved every loose thing in its path, and caused a stinging cloud of dust. The sky to the west turned orange. Then a large hole appeared in the clouds over Nagasaki, showing a clear blue area of sky. A strange-looking, snowy-white mushroom-shaped cloud rose out of that orange base. The cloud climbed higher and higher, mushrooming out as it rose.

Someone remarked, "Man, what a blast!" Another voice said, "Must have hit a big ammunition dump." We had no idea how powerful it really was, or that we were witnessing the blast of an atomic bomb. It was "Fat Boy," the second atomic bomb, a plutonium bomb that had just been dropped from a B-29, the *Superfortres* "Bock's Car," at 11 a.m. Japanese time. It flattened the center of Nagasaki and reportedly killed some thirty-five thousand people.

We returned to our barracks to get some sleep, not knowing that we had just witnessed the beginning of the end of World War II—the greatest conflict in history, in which some fifty-five million died and some three million were missing in action. The war had lasted five long years. But we were not out yet.

Work continued at the mine until August 15, 1945, Japanese time. Our rations had been restored to the same amount as before they had threatened to give us no more food. At 1:30 p.m. that day, we were all brought up from the mine with no explanation. It was a relief to come up, because we were concerned that they might blast the mine shut and entomb us there.

Japanese General Tojo and his military cabinet had controlled the Japanese people in the name of the "Emperor God," Hirohito. The emperor was to be worshipped, but he had a very small part in how the country was run.

The military cabinet controlled the education of the people, young and old alike. They made the laws, and they enforced them under the strict rules of *bushido*, the traditional samurai code of honor, discipline, and morality. Any violation called for strict and severe punishment. To die for this cause was the greatest honor one could obtain. To die for any other reason was a wasted life. There was little or no value placed on an individual's life.

On August 15, 1945, the emperor spoke to his people. This was a first. To them it was their god speaking. He had told them that the war was over and that to continue to fight would only lead to obliteration of the Japanese people. He had come forth and overruled the military cabinet. It was a dangerous move for him.

Although this seemed to please some of the guards, others had a glare of hatred in their eyes. It was obvious that they were ready to charge us with bayonet or sword to get in their last revenge and, hopefully, save face. It could have easily turned into a massacre. There were some very tense moments. We didn't know from one moment to the next whether we would live or die. The Japs didn't know either.

Chapter XII

The Food Drop

I cannot recall what all went on in camp between August 15 and the last half of the month, when American planes started dropping food for us. I do well remember the thrill and excitement in camp as those beautiful planes came, slow and low, dropping the barrels of food. "Manna from Heaven," we called it. We all freaked out.

Some barrels were on wooden pallets, others in web belts, all on parachutes. Some planes came in so low and slow that the chutes barely had time to open before the barrels hit the ground. They hit with such force that some burst open, scattering candy bars and cans of all kinds of good U.S. food.

As food started to pile up, there was a change in the discipline of the guards. Some had disappeared. Others seemed to become more human. They still carried their guns, but most of them stayed just outside of camp, watching sights they had never seen before. One came in and even offered to give his rifle to someone, saying, "You and I are now friends." That was a quick turnabout from the beatings and torture.

Along with all good there always seems to be some sadness. As those food-drop planes came over, they first flew a circle over camp to alert us as to what they were going to do so that we could clear the drop area. Then on the second time around, coming in slow and low, they would make their drop.

Even then some of our guys would run out under these fifty-five-gallon drums. I saw one man run under a descending drum with outstretched arms yelling, "This one is mine." He caught it right in the chest. It smashed him into the ground, killing him instantly. There were other casualties after the war had ended.

One plane, a big B-29, was so low and slow that we could see the pilot waving at us. His wheels were down for drag. He dumped his load then revved the engines, but it was too late. As he turned to miss the nearby mountain, the big plane sideslipped, catching and tearing off the right wing. As it crashed there was an explosion and a ball of flame. I'm quite sure no one survived. It was the pilot's last good deed.

Our men in charge of camp wanted all of the barrels taken to the kitchen for distribution, but it didn't all get there. With all that food, we gorged. Each man became an instant connoisseur of concoctions. We guarded our pile of goodies with one eye on the guards and an eye on our fellow prisoners. We were like wolves at a kill. But still there was no word that any of our troops were landing. We had no place to go. I made a little blackjack out of a part of an old belt laced together and filled with rocks.

On September 10, the guards at the gate screamed, "*Kyotski!*" and bowed as a war correspondent walked in. (If I remember right, he was from the *Chicago Daily News.*) He was after red-hot news for his paper. He called us all around him and got up on the commander's platform. I thought, "Poor man, we are going to see another beheading."

He told us that the war was over. That Japan had surrendered. After we stopped cheering, he went on to tell us that no American troops had landed as yet, but that a small group of army engineers were on the very southern tip of the island that we were on. He said that they were fixing up a landing field so that big planes could bring in troops and supplies. These engineers had come in on C-47 planes. He had come in with them.

When he mentioned that the airport was near the town of Kanoyo, about 150 miles south of where we were, I noted it. He also said that no one had attempted to harm him on the way up, and that it would be two or three weeks before anyone would be in to transport us out. He went on to say that President Roosevelt had died, and that we had a new president by the name of Harry Truman. No one had ever heard of Harry Truman.

I knew where there was a loose board in the twelve-foot-high fence, and I figured that if the reporter had come through unharmed, I could make it out the same way. Early the next morning I slipped out through the narrow space. As I stood there in the open, getting my bearings, a guard came around the corner with rifle and fixed bayonet. He looked straight at me and then turned and went back around the corner. I thought he must be checking to see that his gun was loaded.

    Not knowing just what he would do, my feet took over, and I found myself making a mad dash for a nearby house that had a bicycle leaning against it. I leaped on the bike and started peddling for all I was worth. I knew I couldn't outrun his bullets, but I prayed he would be a poor shot. I zigzagged and headed down between a row of buildings in the direction from which we had heard the trains.

Only a few people were up at that hour. Those I passed stared. Seeing a near-naked white man on a bicycle, racing as though the devil was after him, was no doubt an unusual sight.

Arriving at the train depot that morning, I immediately hid the bike in a patch of shrubbery and stood behind a clump of trees. My thought was that I would jump the first train heading south and take my chances that it would take me to Kanoyo. I waited and waited. All trains were going north. I began to wonder if it was a one-way track.

There was a school-type bench at the near end of the depot platform. On it sat an old Japanese man all alone. My mind flashed back to the bum on the San Francisco docks back in early October of 1941.

Could it be the same man? He looked so small now, so thin and helpless, so old and wrinkled. But he did have a long, thin stick in his hand. I would try to talk to him. It would be worth a try. I could whip him if it came to it. I still had my little blackjack tucked under my G-string.

I eased over and quietly sat down near him. He acted as though he wasn't aware that I was there. Then, after a long wait, and without looking in my direction he said, "*Horyo ka?*" He was asking if I was a prisoner. I replied, "*Ush.*" He asked where I was going, and I told him Kanoyo.

He remained silent for a long time as he smoothed the dust on the ground in front of him with his stick. Then he started marking out something. I watched with interest. It soon took the shape of the island we were on,

Kyushu. Then he punched a place on his dirt map and said, "Omuta," the town we were in.

I realized then that he might be friendly. He drew a wiggly line down to the south end, punched a spot, and said, "Kanoyo." He then said, "*Nee-bon tincho,*" the number two train. I concluded, incorrectly, that the second train to arrive would be my train. I turned to ask him what time it would come, but he was nowhere around. He'd completely disappeared.

I wanted to make a copy of the map. I had a stub of a pencil in the tie-string of my G-string but no paper. On the windowsill of the train depot building was a little stack of toilet paper held down with a brick. I took one of these and sketched his map.

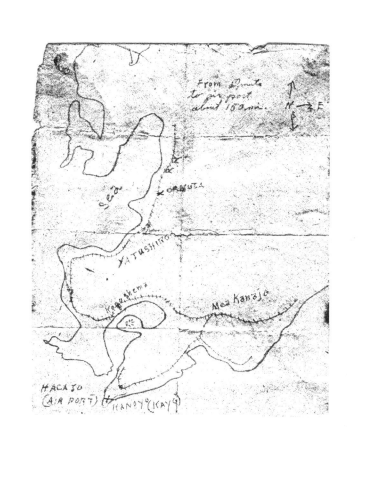

Another train came in from the south, paused for a moment, and then went on its way to the north. Soon another train blasted its whistle. It was coming from the north. This could be that second train. I hurried to the tracks, but it didn't even slow down. Maybe the old man hated naked white men.

Time passed slowly. Late in the afternoon another train came from the north. It had to be the one. It slowed down, but what was I seeing? I blinked my eyes to make sure. Yes, it was a Japanese Army train loaded with soldiers.

As the train came to a stop, a whistle blew, and they came pouring out in full combat gear—rifles, bayonets, hand grenades, steel helmets, and everything else. Some carried machine guns and boxes of ammunition. I faded back into my clump of trees. If I could find that old man I would wring his neck. Perhaps I had made a dumb move and should have stayed in camp with the others.

A whistle blew again, and they all lined up for roll call and reported in. An officer rattled off a bunch of instructions to them with something about chow. He then dismissed them, and they stacked their arms. I watched where they placed the machine guns and boxes of ammunition. I would at least go out fighting.

They lined up and drew their chow from the train car kitchen, returned, and sat down by their guns to eat.

By now it was quite dark. Soon there was another whistle blast. They all jumped up, grabbed their guns, loaded onto the train, and were off in a cloud of steam and coal smoke with a long eerie blast from the train's whistle.

They were gone, and I was still there. It became very quiet. The night air had a chill in it. I was hungry and thirsty. I curled up on the little school bench and fell asleep.

Chapter XIII

Number Two Train

The shrill blast of a locomotive whistle brought me to my feet. The place was crowded with civilians. There were hundreds of them, mostly women and children. What men there were, were either very young or very old. They had bundles of their worldly possessions with them, including some live chickens.

A bright light from the approaching train flashed back and forth. It seemed very bright on this dark night. As I shaded my eyes with my hand, I saw, under the headlight, the Japanese character for the number two, an equal sign. This, then, was the number two train the old man had told me about.

The civilians pushed and crowded to gain a better position for boarding. I found myself being forced farther and farther back. It was obvious that there were far more people than could possible get on. I wouldn't stand a chance. I had a drained feeling. What now?

As the train came to a squealing halt there was a mad clamor to get aboard. In no time, every car was packed with people. Even the back platform of the caboose was packed. Some were standing on the step, and some were hanging on the pipe rails. Many more wanted to get on.

The train started to build up steam again, and the wheels started to slowly turn. A voice behind me startled me with *Hoyoka.* I turned to see one of the tallest Japanese I had seen so far. He was a good six feet six inches tall. He was in military uniform and wore a wide armband on his sleeve, showing that he was one of the military police. I said that I was, and he motioned me to hurry on.

I raised my arms in despair, and told him in Japanese that there was no room for me. He then pulled out his whistle and gave three loud blasts and waved at the flagman. The train came to a stop. He then walked up to those on the back deck and said something to them. No one moved. The MP then went into a burst of rage and drawing out his long billy club proceeded to beat on everyone within striking distance. He hit them hard, with full swings. They scattered like chaff in the wind. He not only cleared off the back deck but also chased out everyone in the back part of the caboose, including everyone on the back two bench seats.

    Then he came back out and motioned me to board. I saluted him, and he bowed in return. I had to put on a show of importance, so I strutted on in. Everyone turned their face away from me, a sign of respect that they also showed to their emperor. I was impressed. The train pulled out. I was finally on my way.

    The little train steamed along through the night, blasting its whistle as it approached every tunnel, and there were many. Soot, cinders, and smoke whirled through the small open windows. It wasn't long before all aboard were coated with soot and smelled of sulfur fumes.

My eyes burned, and I joined the others in coughing spells. It was a grim reminder of the long hours I had spent in the coal mine. My headache returned and the continuous swaying motion didn't help the nauseous feeling of my empty stomach.

One of those who were standing was a very old and apparently quite ill Japanese woman. She was very stooped, and her knobby hands told of arthritis and years of hard work. She was holding two buff-red chickens by their legs, heads down. They were very much alive and kept staring at me. Saliva dripped from their beaks. The poor old woman looked as though she might pass out. The two back benches of the caboose car were empty, except for me.

I called to her in Japanese and asked her to have a seat. This was a terrible mistake on my part. Something you just don't do in Japan. I didn't know it at the time, but it could have cost me my life. It was a direct violation of Japanese protocol.

That Japanese MP had placed me higher on the social ladder than anyone there. Now I had lowered myself lower than the peasant women, even lower than an old sick one who was at the very bottom of the social structure, one who was only entitled to half rations because she was of no further use to the country or her emperor.

Hisses and mumbling ran through the crowd. They glared at me. One woman spit on me. The old woman whom I had tried to befriend wouldn't come near me. She was well aware of the rules. I was lower than dirt. They immediately filled the two benches and jammed tight against me with indignation.

The train stopped at a little town and a number of them got off. That was a big relief. At another stop a couple of ex-POWs got on. They couldn't speak any English, but it was sure good to have them along.

After a few more stops all of the civilians had gotten off, and only myself and the other POWs were left. I dozed off. Sometime in the early morning of the next day, September 12, the train came to an abrupt stop. I woke with a start. The moon was shining in through the little train window. Silhouetted against it was the head of a soldier looking in. He was wearing a helmet that looked to me like a Nazi helmet. My confused thought was, "How could I have arrived in Germany, another prison camp?" Then a booming voice called out, "Are there any American POWs in there?" I saw he was wearing a shoulder patch that read, "Ranger."

My emotions were uncontrollable. I leaped through that tiny window like squirting a watermelon seed, landing right in that poor guy's arms, scaring him half to death.

What could he do with a dirty, smelly, near-naked skeleton? He dropped me and backed off, no doubt wondering what in the world I was. I had been a prisoner of war for 1,226 days.

After adjusting to the shock of seeing such a sight, he and the others of the welcoming party got us into an army Jeep and took us to their mess kitchen. A lieutenant met us there and told us that they had heard there were a number of POWs on that train and they had food ready for all of us. He said that after we got filled up a doctor would check us over.

Food was what I wanted, so I made my way to the small cook shack. It had one room, divided down the center by a low deck-type railing. In the divider was a swinging gate. Just beyond were some of the fattest cooks I had ever seen. They were dressed in white, clean cook outfits. Their shining faces beamed with pleasure as they saw my scrawny body.

Bubbling on the stoves behind them were large pots of oatmeal and beef-vegetable stew. Sizzling on the griddle were scrambled eggs and bacon. Through the glass of an oven door, a big pan of golden corn bread was visible. I could smell the hot chocolate and fresh coffee.

On a nearby table were opened gallon cans of jam, peaches, fruit cocktail, and apple butter.

Well trained from years in prison camp where rushing for your food cost you that ration, I stood in trembling excitement with bulging eyes and dripping mouth, focused on that apple butter.

Some one called out, "Well what are you waiting for? There's enough here for a hundred of you." I jumped the railing, grabbed a big spoon and a gallon of apple butter, dropped down on the floor cross-legged, and started shoveling it in as fast as my arm would bend. The cooks stared. I don't know what they were thinking.

After having gulped down most of it, I had to stop because I couldn't swallow any more and my stomach was starting to hurt. But it was a very good kind of a hurt.

Someone said something like, "What are we going to do with the rest of this stuff?"

Slowly I got up and looked down at my bulging stomach that was protruding from my skeleton frame. It reminded me of a grape pierced by a toothpick. Definitely not a very flattering physique. Exiting by way of the little gate, I thanked them. As I left, someone sang out, "There's plenty of seconds."

Outside there three company men were waiting for me. They escorted me down to the shower area. Barrels had been suspended at a height of about six feet. A spray faucet and control valve had been installed at the base of each. They were full of water that had been warmed by the sun. The big bars of yellow soap reminded me of the old homemade soap we made back on the folks' farm. It had been made from animal fat and lye leached from wood ashes. The soap stung the many cuts and sores of feet and body.

A corpsman dusted me with some kind of yellow powder and weighed me. The scales balanced at 103 pounds, an increase of 6 pounds since the food drop had started just two weeks before.

The doctor checked me over, treated my open sores, and gave me pills and a vaccination of some kind. He said I seemed to be in fair condition considering what I had been going through over the last four years.

The lieutenant came by and told me that he and the men had just had a meeting and they had unanimously agreed that all of us who had been prisoners could join them in their barracks, could take over any bunk we wanted, could have any of their clothing and toilet articles we wanted, and they would consider it an honor to share these things with us. They couldn't have been more generous. They had many questions. It was dark when I hit the bunk and dropped off into a peaceful and deep sleep.

I was awakened by a gentle shake from the lieutenant. It was still dark. He said, "There is a plane leaving for the island of Okinawa. The pilot said he would wait for anyone who wanted to go along." I said yes and sprang to my feet, thanked him, and was on my way.

By jeep it was a short ride to the plane. I crawled aboard and met the pilot, Lieutenant Warden. He said we would have to wait just a little because there was some small arms firing not far away that was being checked out and also that a low fog was obstructing the view of the holes in the runway.

It must have been somewhere around nine o'clock when we finally were able to get airborne. As the C-47 Jungle Skipper cleared the runway and gained altitude over the deep-blue China Sea, the pilot asked if I would like to move up so that I could see better.

I did, and when I looked out, I saw a perfect circle rainbow. It followed us just below and to the right of the plane. A lump came in my throat and tears to my eyes. I prayed a silent prayer of thanks to God. I looked down again, and what I saw made me blink again and again to make sure of what I was seeing. Forming around the first was a second perfect circle rainbow, both then became very bright and beautiful, projected over the deep blue of the China Sea.

Wondering if it was real or just my imagination I turned to Lieutenant Warden and asked what he saw below us. He glanced down and replied, "A rainbow."

Not satisfied with that answer I persisted, "See anything unusual?"

He glanced again, "It's a double, and they're round."

I slid back to my seat, trembling. No words could begin to tell what a great feeling was within me. I was alive! I was free! I was going home!

Two hours flight time brought us to Okinawa, the island where so many of our fighting men had died. Our pilot brought the plane down in a smooth and perfect landing. We thanked him for bringing us out of the hands of hell. He laughed and assured us it was his pleasure.

As we crawled out of the plane, we came face to face with women. These were real, honest-to-goodness Red Cross women. All smiles, they came rushing toward us with open arms.

I panicked. I hadn't seen any women for over three and a half years. I was so frightened at the sight of them that I turned on my heels and crawled back into the plane. I kept thinking, how awful I must look, and why would they ever want to see me.

Lieutenant Warden asked them to back off, explaining that it would take a little time for us to adjust to normal again. They seemed to understand. After some persuasion from the lieutenant, he and I came back out with his arm around my shoulders. I sure felt ashamed and stupid.

These women had brought out hot coffee, coca cola, candy bars, cigarettes, and even a doughnut machine, and they were making hot fresh doughnuts for us. They were very sympathetic and soon had me tamed down and talking a little. It wasn't easy. The other POWs fared just about as bad. We were like wild animals.

Army trucks were there waiting for us. They took us into camp. Everyone had questions. We cleaned up, got more shots, were checked over and issued a complete outfit of clothing, including a new mess kit with a lid.

We lined up for chow and the men insisted that we all go to the head of the line. I remember they had fried chicken, mashed potatoes, gravy, and green beans (I had the servers dump all of this in my mess kit in that order), topped with pudding and then ice cream. One of the servers suggested that I come back for the ice cream but I said, "No way, just put it on top, and I'll eat that first." He did, and I did.

XIV

Back to the Philippines

At three o'clock in the morning on September 14, we were called out, fed again, and ushered onto a B-24 bomber heading for the Philippines. Five hours flying time brought us to Clark Field at noon. The Red Cross met us again and served each of us a hot lunch. By now I was able to carry on a normal conversation. They had many questions about how we had been treated.

I can't remember just how we got from Clark field to the rehabilitation center south of Manila, my mind was whirling with so many new things and changes. Manila had been bombed to the point that many old landmarks were gone. Filipinos cheered as we went by. They seemed to know that we were the ones who had been there at the beginning of the war. They had lost a lot of their menfolk and family members. They knew what we had been through, and we knew what suffering they had endured. An eternal bond had been forged between us. I did notice that the old Chinese restaurant, where we had been served the cat dinner, was now under a pile of rubble.

It was late when we arrived at the rehabilitation and embargo center. The tent city was large. There were now stockpiles of supplies and foods of all kinds. All of those torturous and horrible days and nights were now behind us. The tension of war was gone. Best of all was the great feeling of freedom, that good feeling that comes when each is recognized as an individual with equal rights under the Constitution. That is a feeling that often is not fully appreciated until deprived.

I gave a prayer of thanks to God for giving me the strength to endure all those days of suffering. I asked his blessing on all of those who had given their lives so that others could continue to have that freedom. Those who can never return are the true heroes. Bless them all.

Each of us was allowed to send one free cablegram home. I sent one to my mother and dad. There was a mail distribution and a letter for me from my brother. It was full of family news. Although it was now late, I started a letter to him. I was too hyped up to sleep. My brother saved that letter and let it be published in several newspapers back home.

September 14, 1945

Dear Brother, Sis, Larry, and Diana:

Free! Free! Free! I give thanks to God most high, who has heard and answered the prayers of my loved ones back home. I can't express in words the feeling that swells inside of me so I won't even attempt it. I got here at midnight last night. Was only allowed one free radiogram (haven't any pay as yet), and I sent it to the folks knowing that you all would get it anyway. So here comes the follow up letter. My mind is going in circles, and I don't know where to begin.

Your letter of September 6th was here waiting for me. Today is the first chance I've had to communicate to you, I came here so fast.

I have been working in a coal mine in the Japanese city of Omuta on the third largest island in Japan. We knew nothing, heard nothing, and were treated worse than dogs. There were 1,734 men in this camp. Some English, some Dutch, some were Australians, Americans, and Javanese native troops (Black).

At 1:30 p.m., Jap time, on August 15, all work was suddenly stopped at the mine, and we were brought up and sent back to camp with no explanation of any kind. I wanted to believe that the war was over but dared not. The meager ration of boiled rice and soup of boiled potato leaves (no potatoes) was increased in amount. We waited. Near the end of the month, American B-29 planes came over and dropped us tons of food. We knew then that the war was over but no more.

On September the 10th, just five days ago, the foreign war correspondent of the Chicago Daily News came into camp from apparently nowhere getting "red hot news" for his paper, and called us all around him. He got up on a platform and told us everything that had been going on. Poor fellow, I'll bet he answered a million questions but asked almost as many of us about our treatment and food, etc.

    He told us that as yet no American troops had landed on this island but a few engineers and smaller planes were fixing up a little landing field at the extreme south end of the island for the troops and big planes to come in. He said the airport was near the town of Kanoyo. I at once wrote down the name. He said it was about 150 miles. I wrote that down too. And he said it would be a few weeks yet before they could get in to us and transport us out.

The next night (Sept. 11th, just four nights back) I skipped camp and headed south with only a little black-jack I had made and this little map you will find enclosed for my guide. (Please take good care of this little map.) This island is the third largest of the Japanese islands. I haven't looked up the name of it yet.

I met other POWs from other camps on the way down, and we all joined together. We arrived at the airport at 8:30 p.m. of the 12th, and saw our first free American soldiers. What a welcome we received. I'll never forget it. And what a feast we had that night. There were some Rangers there. We had a great time together. I drank good G.I. coffee until it nearly ran out of my ears. What a night. I had been a prisoner for three years, four months, and four days.

I left there at dawn the next morning on one of the Jungle Skippers, (C-47) flown by Lieutenant Warden. He took us to Okinawa. We reached there in two hours. They knew we were coming, and the Red Cross met us on the field with all the Cocoa-Colas, candy bars, doughnuts, and coffee we could eat and all the cigarettes we wanted. The Army had trucks there at the field waiting for us and took us into camp. We threw away our rags, cleaned up, and were decked out in new clean cloths and were given everything we needed. At three o'clock the nest morning we were waked up, fed, "babied" and sent back to the field to catch B-24s to the Philippines. Arrived at Clark Field at noon. Five hours flying time. The Red Cross was there again with a hot lunch to meet us. We then went over to one of the *companies and good old Uncle Sam had another big dinner for us. Incidentally I have gained 22 lbs. in the last 27 days and am still gaining fast. Hope to be back to weight soon. Was down to 103 pounds last winter. Must close and get another exam. Will write more later. God be with you all.*

—Clarence

The fact that I had been down to 103 pounds last winter was correct but that had not been my lowest weight by any means. I didn't want to give him that weight, at least not at that time.

The mess halls were open to us twenty-four hours a day. If they didn't have what we wanted, they said, all we had to do was tell them and they would specially prepare it. But they already had everything we could want.

I sat down on the bench at one of the many tables with my plate loaded. Just as I started to shovel it in a young woman sat down beside me, wearing a soldier's uniform. I wondered why she was wearing it. Her plate was nearly as full as mine. She filled her uniform to the uncomfortable point, perhaps a good 100 pounds heavier than I.

    She introduced herself as a WAC and gave her name. As she squeezed her body close to mine, the smell of her perfume and perspiration overpowered that of my food. Immediately she opened a one-sided conversation with many questions about how we had been treated and what the slave labor was like.

I was scared, self-conscious, and embarrassed. Now that I look back at this, she really was very pleasant and just wanted to know how bad life in prison camp had been, but I wasn't able to cope with such a change at that time.

At any rate, food stuck in my throat. I went into a coughing fit, excused myself, left my food, and returned to my army cot, wondering what in the world was wrong with me. After my shaking let up I walked over to the PX stand and asked if I could have a candy bar on credit because I hadn't received any back pay yet. (It had been three years and nine months since my last pay.)

The man there said, "Sure, it's all on Uncle Sam for you guys. What kind do you like?"

"A Hershey without nuts," I said. "My teeth are bad." He shoved a full carton of them over to me and a full carton of Milky Ways, saying, "When you want more, come back."

    I spent the next day with the medical staff. They had a big, long tent that was divided into little examining compartments. A specialist was in each. They took blood samples, urine and stool samples, skin samples, checked ears, eyes, nose, teeth, heart, lungs, feet, and everything else they could think of. Then came the shots and the vaccinations. I was warned by each as I progressed along the way that what they had done to me was nothing like what they were going to do to me at the last compartment. My guess was that it would be a spinal shot of some kind. I was glad that none of them were Japanese doctors.

With aching arms and dabbed with ointments and disinfectants, I paused in front of the last place, wondering if maybe I could skip it. But there was a doctor standing there with an evil smile on his face who said, "This is the last one. Come on in and get it over with."

I thought, what the heck, if it kills me at least I'll die with a full stomach. I went in, and he pulled up a three-legged stool and told me to sit down. Then he poured me a shot glass full of good bourbon saying, "Here is your last shot. You have earned it."

A day or two later I decided to see what remained of the city of Manila. By now I had received a small amount of back pay, plenty for a day of sightseeing. Not having transportation of my own I approached a soldier in a jeep. He was reading a sexy magazine.

"Hi, Joe," I said. (All soldiers were called Joe in the Philippines.) He replied, "You one of those guys who was in a prison camp?"

"Yes, How about a ride downtown?"

"Can you drive a jeep?"

"Sure," I replied.

"They told us that you guys could have anything you want. Can you have it back here before dark?"

"You bet." As he crawled out, he handed me the key and said, "Park it back here when you get back. Don't bang it up or my ass will be mud."

It felt good to be behind the wheel again. The jeep was like new and the gauge showed that it had a full tank of fuel. It was a beautiful day. There was a bright sun and a refreshing breeze from the bay. I was in a new, well-fitting uniform with my new sergeant's stripes on each arm and seven overseas hash marks on my left sleeve. Even had the USAFE Sea Lion shoulder patch on my left shoulder. I felt that I had the world by the tail.

Driving the war-torn streets of that once beautiful city was a real challenge. Shell holes pockmarked the roads. Concrete debris made most streets a real obstacle course.

The native people looked so depressed and poorly clothed it was saddening. But when they saw me they waved and shouted, "Welcome back Bataan man." Little children with bright eyes and big smiles would hold up the two-finger V for victory sign and shout, "Hi, Joe!" What a fine race of people they are.

I drove by the area where, in peacetime, the beautiful and luxurious Metro Gardens had been. There was such destruction that I couldn't get oriented. I asked a young boy who was playing there, "Where is Metro Gardens." His reply was, "Right here but when the Americans came back they took it away. Boom!"

There were a lot of little makeshift stands along the way. Some sold mangoes and papayas. Some had trinkets and clothing. At one stand was a very pretty Filipino girl. She smiled and waved and said, "Welcome back Corregidor soldier." It was amazing how they could spot that Sea Lion shoulder patch. I stopped the jeep by her stand. She came out and threw her arms around me and, giving me a kiss on the cheek, said, "You ask me to go to the States with you, I go. My family all dead now." This was more scary than my encounter with the WAC.

I politely explained that it was not allowed and that I had to get right back to camp. She took a bead necklace from around her neck and held it out for me to take. She said, "This is all I have from my mother. I want you to have it." Tears filled my eyes as I told her that I couldn't take it, that it was something that she should never part with. She started to cry, and I drove off feeling really rotten.

Back at camp I parked the jeep and decided I would never go back to Manila again. I just wanted to get back home. I went to a movie that night, but I can't remember what it was about. Things were bothering me too much. It was hard to readjust.

I ate and slept and ate, went to movies, and ate some more. Under my bunk was a continually growing stash of food. All of us were doing this. In twenty-seven days I gained twenty-two pounds and never got sick.

We were given a choice of going home by flying back in one of the war-torn bombers that were returning to the States to be put in mothballs or taking the safer choice of returning by boat. I chose the latter.

It was October 1, 1945, that my ship headed out from the Philippines on the return to the States. We were assigned bunks below deck, and when I went down into those packed, smelly quarters it brought back all those horrible memories of the days in the coal mine. Just as soon as the ladder was clear of entering ex-POWs I hauled my gear back up and took residence in one of the lifeboats.

A man from my old outfit joined me, and we started stashing a supply of food again. We made a list of the men from our battery who we knew were killed in action. We attempted to list those who died from tortures and those who had died from starvation and/or diseases. We had to give up on making the last list because of our limited knowledge. There were too many camps and no way of knowing who was where.

I did make notes of times and places of events so that I could write a book some day. The book—this book—was a long time in coming. But it is the true story of what I saw and what I experienced.

Life on the ship was boring. I don't know how sailors can stand it. It seemed forever to get back. There was nothing to do but look out over the water, think of home, and watch a movie at night.

On October 15, 1945, we sailed back under the Golden Gate Bridge, ending four years, six months, and five days overseas, and nearly six years service time, all on just one three-year enlistment. But I was one of the lucky ones. I was coming back.

What a thrill it was as that monstrous ship glided silently under the Golden Gate Bridge and entered the quiet waters of San Francisco Bay. It was a beautiful day. A soft breeze fluffed out the folds of the Stars and Stripes above us. I saluted it. "Long may it live," I thought. I also thought about all of those who would never see it again, those who had given their lives so that we could enjoy the freedom of our great nation. God bless them all. I swallowed hard but the lump in my throat would not move.

Numerous boats were in the bay to welcome us home. Balloons flew, music played, and a special welcoming ship loaded with cheering and waving people was there to escort us to the docks.

My wish was, and is to this day, that everyone in the United States could appreciate our freedom and this wonderful country as I do.

Thanks to Paul Carter / **The Register Guard** for permission to use this picture.

About the Author

Sergeant Graham, a quiet and patriotic man, married a girl from near his hometown in Nebraska. After his discharge from the Army he was employed by the U.S. Department of Agriculture, Soil Conservation Service where he worked until he retired in 1976. He then worked for a number of years with the Oregon State Parks Service as a Park Ranger. He was also active in the Oregon National Guard Reserves, raising to the rank of Lt. Colonel and commanded the 10th Battalion. Clarence and his wife Doris have been married for more than 50 years. They have four children, a son and three daughters, and ten grandchildren. Clarence has been interviewed and featured in Tom Brokaw's book "The Greatest Generation Speaks" and the NBC Special Unbroken. Now in his mid 90's, it is Clarence's wish to share his story and experience of the War. Through this book his story lives on.

Made in the USA
Las Vegas, NV
04 December 2021